LIFE,
DEATH,
AND
DESTINY

LAYMAN'S THEOLOGICAL LIBRARY
Robert McAfee Brown, *General Editor*

Life,
Death,
and
Destiny

by
Roger Lincoln Shinn

LAYMAN'S
THEOLOGICAL
LIBRARY

THE WESTMINSTER PRESS

PHILADELPHIA

Library of Congress Catalog Card No.: 57–5764

PRINTED IN THE UNITED STATES OF AMERICA

CONTENTS

5

The religious book market is full of books for "the intelligent layman." Some are an insult to his intelligence. Others are covertly written for professional theologians. A few are genuine helps in communicating the faith.

In this spate of books being thrust at the lay reader, what distinctive place can the Layman's Theological Library claim to hold? For one thing, it will try to remind the layman that he *is* a theologian. The close conjunction of the words "layman" and "theological" in the title of the series is not by chance but by design. For theology is not an irrelevant pastime of seminary professors. It is the occupation of every Christian, the moment he begins to think about, or talk about, or communicate, his Christian faith. The injunction to love God *with all his mind,* necessarily involves the layman in theology. He can never avoid theology; if he refuses to think through his faith, he simply settles for an inferior theology.

Furthermore, the Layman's Theological Library will attempt to give a *wholeness* in its presentation of the Christian faith. Its twelve volumes cover the main areas of Christian faith and practice. They are written out of similar convictions which the authors share about the uniqueness of the Christian faith. All the authors are convinced that Christian faith can be made relevant, that it can be made understandable without becoming innocuous, and that (particularly in view of the current "return to religion") it is crucially important for the

7

layman to commit himself to more than " religion in general."
The Layman's Theological Library, then, will attempt a fresh
exploration of the Christian faith and what it can mean in the
life of twentieth-century man.

There may be some questions that are " academic questions " in the sense that they do not really concern our inner-
most selves, but none of the questions we ask about " life,
death, and destiny " can ever remain academic.

Whenever we wonder whether our life really adds up to
anything; whenever we ask ourselves about death, particularly our own death; whenever we begin to doubt, or hope,
that we have a destiny greater than either life or death — then
we are caught up in the questions and issues with which the
following pages deal.

Some Christians move with such detailed confidence in
these areas that we begin to wonder how they got so much
more inside information than Jesus ever claimed to have, and
we begin to suspect that their guidance is less than fully re-
liable. Other Christians, aware that their vision is less than
total, give up the attempt to deal with the questions, and leave
us with a " faith " that lacks any content.

Dr. Shinn's treatment, on the contrary, will give real help
to the reader who is concerned to discover what the resources
of Christian faith have to say to him when he asks the really
basic questions he cannot avoid asking, and who can also
appreciate the combination of modesty and courage that is
involved in acknowledging both that we see through a glass
darkly, and that nevertheless there are even now some things
that we *do see,* even though we are not yet face to face.

ROBERT McAFEE BROWN

1

A Mystery and a Clue

. . . The war was almost over. News of the armistice had reached the troops, but the actual order to cease fire was still on the way to the front. Then a bursting shell tore open a soldier's flesh. As his blood flowed out of the fatal wound, the man said, "Isn't this just like God?"

. . . A member of a President's cabinet resigned after two and a half years in office. After accepting the President's thanks, the Secretary responded, "I truly feel that God has had his hand on the United States in the kind of leadership you have given us."

. . . A farmer in California's Imperial Valley irrigation area told a traveler: "It used to be, when we needed rain, we prayed for it. Now we telephone."

. . . An author, presenting his program for world peace, stated that all the achievements of mankind had so far done nothing to eliminate wars. The furious conflicts of the twentieth century, he said, prove "the complete bankruptcy of Christianity as a civilizing force."

. . . A famous political speaker told his audience that the United States could surely outlast Russia because our spiritual values are superior to Communist atheism. Then he proposed an armaments program to insure national security. One listener commented, "I wonder why he thinks we need the second if he's so sure of the first."

. . . Voltaire said, "God is on the side of the heaviest battalions." Napoleon, who agreed, located God "on the side of the last reserve."

. . . But Victor Hugo wrote that it was impossible for Napoleon to win at Waterloo — not because of the opposing armies but because of God. "The hour had come for supreme incorruptible Justice to take notice. Napoleon had been denounced in the Infinite and his downfall had been determined."

What do these paragraphs have in common? They all touch on the same subject. They show how people in various situations think about God's ways with men. They express some faith or some challenge to the faith that God is Lord of life and of death.

During the next month, if you want to, you can pile up a hundred more paragraphs like those above. For every day editorials, speeches, offhand remarks around home or work or church deal with this issue. We all have our purposes, our hopes, our plans for reaching goals. And we all wonder how our own activities fit into the larger operations around us. Most of us, sooner or later, ask whether God really runs this world and whether he does anything about human affairs. We ask whether he inflicts death, or stands helplessly by when we die, or — as some faiths proclaim — conquers death.

The Mystery of Our History

All religions have something to say about these questions. But they do not all agree. Their answers cover just about all the possibilities, and they cannot all be right.

Among the many religions of mankind, Judaism and Christianity belong to the very small group known as "historical religions." Their Bible is a long book that tells the story of the Jewish people and the early years of the Christian people. It has no chapter labeled " God: How He Deals with Human Life and Death." Instead, it seems to say to us: " If you want to learn about this subject, read here the history of these people. Here you will see God working among men."

But if we accept the invitation, we find an unusual kind of history. True, it tells about a lot of people doing things — adventuring, lusting, warring, dreaming, eating, forgiving, bleeding, worshiping, dying. All these things, we know, happen in the history of any people. But nobody is likely to confuse the Bible with any normal history book that the children bring home from school.

We need those schoolbooks about history. They have important purposes. The Bible won't take their place. But as soon as we start talking about the Bible and the schoolbooks as histories we realize that the word " history " hides a lot of difficulties. For a word that is used so often, " history " is a slippery one. Can we say what it means?

One brilliant American historian, Carl Becker, has defined history as " the memory of things said and done." Immediately someone says: " That won't do. Memories are inaccurate and incomplete. History is what *really happened*."

That comment has its place. When we ask whether George Washington actually cut down the cherry tree or threw the silver dollar across the Rappahannock River, we are trying to get to the facts. We are aiming to correct faulty memories — no longer individual memories, of course, but memories of a society. This drive for accuracy is all to the good.

But now we run into trouble. The truth is that nobody knows all the original facts. And nobody wants to know them all. It is impossible to remember or record all the " things said and done " in a single day in the life of one city — or even one person. Maybe it all belongs to history. Practically, only part of it is important enough to belong to *the history that concerns us.*

But now the word "history" gets still more perplexing. Granting that many things are not important enough to bother about, let's say that we still want to know "what really happened," not what somebody dreams or wishes had happened. How do we find out what happened?

Suppose, to take an example, you want to settle a bet. You need to know what major-league baseball player had the highest batting average in 1945, or what was the hottest day in Los Angeles in 1950, or what was the Federal budget in 1955. A little research will turn up the answer. Definite facts are available. If you know how to get at the data, you will settle the issue — even if the facts force you to admit that you have been mistaken.

But what have you accomplished? You have secured accurate information about a little slice of history. You still have not learned much about history.

Now expand the example. Suppose you want to find out all you can about the 1945 baseball season. You want your knowledge to be accurate and objective. What do you do? Maybe you collect the statistics on batting and pitching and fielding, on games won and lost, on gate receipts and games postponed because of bad weather. You get the data on home and road games, night and day games, single games and doubleheaders. Of course you disregard all memories of partisan fans, because they are prejudiced. You accept only the verifiable facts — and you get thousands of them. You assemble these facts, organize them, make calculations about them or feed them into an electronic computer and get out all sorts of correlations you hadn't noticed before.

Still you don't have a history of that baseball season. You

have missed the drama and excitement that make baseball what it is in American life. For the sake of objectivity you have left out the bias of the fans — but the partisanship of the fans of the Brooklyn Dodgers or Cleveland Indians is itself one of the facts about any baseball season. To avoid prejudice you left out the subjective attitudes of the players toward their managers — but those subjective feelings became objective factors that won and lost games. You finally discover that the season cannot be reported in terms of facts and computations on the machine. You understand the history of that season only when *honest facts* grasp *human imagination* so that you can somehow relive those past experiences now. Then that history belongs to you and you belong to it.

Now expand the example again. Suppose you consider not just the baseball season but the whole history of 1945. Nobody can come close to assembling all the facts of a single year. It may be that the person who knows the most facts is simply the most confused about what really happened. If we ask how the events of 1945 shaped the destiny of Western civilization or of our personal lives, the answer will not come just by tabulating the data. Only time will tell the full importance of those years. And time will not tell everything.

Yet while we wait for time to tell as much as it will, we go on living and thinking. We know something about those years — as we know something about the history of the ancient Hebrews and Greeks and Romans, or the modern British and Russians and Americans. What we know is due partly to the objective data we can accumulate and organize. It is due partly to the way in which the history of these peoples has shaped our activities and made us what we are.

So the word " history " (throughout this book and in most human thinking) goes deeper than we see at first glance. It includes (1) *what has happened* and — more important —

(2) *what those happenings mean and do to the people who live through them and after them.*

Here, then, is something momentous for our original problem. If we want to know *what God does in history,* we must ask not merely what big events take place; we must reach far enough into human experiences to find *what God does to people* in those events.

That is why we need both the schoolbooks about history and the Bible. The schoolbooks include a lot of information that never got into the Bible. But the Bible tells, as no other book does, of what God does to people in history.

Still, the Bible doesn't tell everything. Over and over again it confesses ignorance. To some of our questions its answer is that we human beings just cannot understand. It proclaims that our history is a mystery.

An Objection and an Answer

It's fair enough at this point to raise an objection to the reasoning that has been going on. The objection runs something like this:

First, you bring up some questions about what God does in human affairs — the affairs of both life and death. You show that people often wrestle with these questions.

Secondly, you say that the Bible of the Jewish and Christian religions meets these questions by telling the history of certain people and showing how God deals with people.

So far, so good — maybe. But then you say that the Bible admits that it can't answer these questions because they are part of a mystery.

Where are we getting? If I'm lost, you don't help me by sending me down a road that ends where I'm still lost.

This objection deserves a hearing. It points to a genuine problem in all attempts to think about human life in terms of the Bible. But that need not stop us. All serious thinking runs into problems. The test is not whether it avoids them or even removes them, but whether it does anything worth-while with them. The answer to this particular difficulty involves two steps.

Step 1. Notice that the problem is not something artificial that comes out of some curious religious teachings. Rather it comes out of the very business of human living. Over and over we try to understand life and to know where it is leading us. And life answers back, *"You can't know, but you have to know."* Maybe this answer looks unfair, but there is no getting around it. Look at both sides of it and see how realistic they are.

"You can't know." You can't look ahead a single year and know with any certainty whether you and your family will be alive. You can't know whether epidemics or H-bombs will be turned loose, whether the world will be getting wiser or heading toward disaster. Make it a question of ten years — or a thousand years — and the doubt gets thicker. Ask about the whole human enterprise, and no one can answer much of anything.

"But you have to know." Your own experience tells you why. *Every decision assumes that you have some notion of what is important and what purposes you want to achieve.* Can you show any sanity in marrying and making a home? Do you have any reasons for the plan of your budget or the use of your time? Only if you have some sense — incomplete, of course, but fairly vivid — of where you are going. Only if you can take some posture, assume some attitudes, maintain some confidence about the goals of life.

That, then, is the way life addresses us. Reasonable or not, it thrusts us into situations where we need to know more than it tells us.

Step 2. Although life does not give us the answers to its mysteries, it does give *some clues*. These clues do not come with printed labels. As in any mystery, some people see clues that others miss. And people argue with each other about which are the real clues.

But clues there are. From them we may gain insight into the question of our destiny. It is time to examine some of these clues.

Clues and the Clue

A publisher, aiming to call attention to a new book, asked a group of prominent people to rate the most important events of the past. The panel of judges — journalists, professors, historians — made their lists. When the results were tabulated, highest honors went to these events: 1. The discovery of America by Columbus. 2. Gutenberg's development of movable type.

Those choices tell us something about history. Maybe they tell us even more about the men who made them. Obviously the panel of experts was loaded with Americans — who were authors and scholars to boot. They had a stake in the discovery of America and the development of the printing press. When they called these events important, they meant important *for them*.

True, these men chose historical events that are important for many people besides themselves. Yet their choices are not *the most important* to everyone. If the leaders of world Communism had voted, they might have specified the Russian Revolution. A skilled technician might point to the time when an unknown savage first learned to control and use fire. Other answers would come from national leaders like George Wash-

ington or Winston Churchill, Pandit Nehru or Premier Chou
En-lai. Still others would come from scientists like Galileo or
Einstein. Albert Schweitzer in Africa or the pope in Rome
might give utterly different replies. Each answer would tell us
something about the events of history *and* something about
the man who answered the question. For our choices are always determined partly by the objective facts and partly by
what these facts have done to us.

Consider two other men who answered a similar question.
The American writer Ernest Hemingway, when asked the
most important date in history, answered, " I have no important dates." It is hard to believe that answer exactly as it
stands. Mr. Hemingway could not be so skillful a storyteller
unless he had a keen power to see what is significant. But he
means to tell us that he sees no one great happening that
throws its influence over all the rest.

By contrast the Italian novelist Ignazio Silone declared that
the most important date of history is " the twenty-fifth of
December, Year Zero." His answer tells us that the birth of
Jesus not only affected the world in important ways but also
means something in the life of Signor Silone.

Here, then, are a few answers to the question of what is
important in history: the discovery of America, the development of movable type, the birth of Jesus, numerous other oc-
currences, . . . or nothing in particular.

Now return to the publisher's poll. It can be reported, for
whatever it is worth, that Jesus did earn a rating. *Behind
thirteen other events,* tied with the discovery of X-ray, the
flight of the Wright brothers' plane, and some more, *came the
crucifixion of Jesus.*

Many people will find something bizarre about this attempt

to put Jesus on the right rung in the ladder of importance. Certainly a Christian will not be content with the judgment that the career of Jesus belongs among the first twenty events of history. He will not be much more pleased to have it pushed up into the top ten — say ahead of X-ray but still behind Columbus and Gutenberg. Third or second place, somehow, is little better. And it is curiously unsatisfying even to argue that Jesus deserves top place on the list.

The trouble is that this whole procedure works on the basis of a doubtful assumption. It says that we look at the history of the human race with a fairly clear knowledge of what is important. We begin with a set of standards for measuring the worth of things, and we fit Jesus and Columbus and the rest into this set of standards. We judge and rate their value. Because these men do things that meet *our* standards of importance, we rate them high.

Actually this kind of thinking is not realistic. We do not approach the world with a built-in measuring rod for sizing up things around us. We do not work with some list of abstract standards that tells us what is important.

On the contrary, our sense of the worth of things depends upon *what has happened to us*. The career of Columbus is not merely something that we find important; his activities have done something momentous to us. They have affected our whole historical heritage, so that our outlook upon the world is influenced by the fact that he discovered this continent.

If so much is true of Columbus, the same is far more decisively true when Christians think about Jesus, whom they call Lord or Christ or Savior. It is unrealistic to say, "We have evaluated the career of Jesus and have found great worthiness here." It is realistic to say: "He has done something to us that changes the way we look at life. He shows us what is worthy."

Hence, looking at history, the Christian does not say, "In the light of my best understanding this strand of history reported in the Bible is the most important." He says, "This strand of history gives me light toward dealing with all the rest."

Of course, all this may be mere pious talk. But if so, it is because we are not really Christian. For the Christian testimony has always been that Jesus Christ changes lives, transforms them, turns them about. The Christian experience is not that of judging the activities of Jesus; it is that of being judged — yes, of being convicted and yet renewed — when confronted by that career.

That is why Christians find in the cluster of events connected with Jesus of Nazareth *the clue* to the mystery of our history. All people, as they stride or stumble through life, rely upon some clues. Christians with the rest of mankind find a great many useful clues. But they find this one peculiarly decisive in letting them see how God deals with men in life and in death.

Naturally no one has to determine his bearings from this clue. But no one has to reject it out of hand merely because it is not the stylish belief in many circles. Actually people live by an amazing variety of beliefs. Faced with so many possibilities, the testimony of the Christian Church is something like this: "In the midst of all that we do not know or understand, we do understand ourselves better because Christ has met us. We know our neighbors better because of him. Our personal history and our whole human history mean something vastly different because of that history of the first few decades after Christ. We have a clue to God's ways with men."

That is the testimony. The least we can do is give it a hearing.

From Clue to Testimony

When the bank statement comes at the end of the month, it sometimes disagrees with the balance on the check stubs. We're annoyed, but we know what to do. We work over the figures, see whether the checks agree with the stubs, do some adding and subtracting. Sooner or later something clears up. Sometimes — not very often — the bank has made a mistake. Sometimes — usually, in fact — we pulled the boner.

In either case we know there is a right answer. It never enters our heads that perhaps we and the bank just cannot agree. Arithmetic has its rules. Everybody who follows the rules has to get the same answers.

But life has other puzzles of a different kind. Sometimes our best friends disagree on how we should face a situation. We want to choose a career, marry the right person, rear our children in the best way. Or we want to vote for competent public officials, support just legislation, back up the wisest foreign policy. In all these decisions intelligence is a great help. But intelligence doesn't guarantee that we'll all come out with the same answer. There are no set rules — like the rules of arithmetic — guaranteed to cover the whole situation.

When we try to understand God's dealings with men, we clearly are not working an arithmetic problem. Men, looking at human history, find many different clues to help them understand it and live in it. This does not mean that all the clues are equally good. It does mean that all of them have some appeal to some people.

We have already seen the reasons. First, so many things happen in history that no one can know all of them or even most of them. We work with a selection from them. Secondly, our response to history depends upon what history has done to us. Hence there is a deeply personal quality about this response, a quality that is irrelevant when we add the figures on the check stubs.

No wonder there are so many arguments over the great questions about the meaning of life and death. Although intelligence alone will not guarantee that we get the right answer, intelligence can be useful. Its first job is to help locate the problem. The better it defines the problem, the better it can see what clues help.

Locating the Problem

"*Man is the only animal that laughs and weeps, since he alone perceives the difference between things as they are and as they ought to be.*" Whatever the case with animals — of which our knowledge is small — this statement from William Hazlitt is clear about human beings.

Laughter is one way of making that *difference* bearable or even enjoyable. Weeping expresses the painfulness of the difference. Sometimes the two come close together. Is it funny or sad to slip on a banana peel? or to get caught in the rain and have our best clothes soaked? or to make a social boner in polite society? It depends on how much these slips hurt and how deeply we are involved. When a writer like Shakespeare intermingles rollicking comedy and intense tragedy in the same play, he shows how men respond with both moods to this continuous difference between what is and what ought to be.

The human race has met this difference in many ways. People have dramatized it in songs and poems and stories. They have turned bitter over it and murdered their enemies. They have taken it as an incentive to make life more bearable through the achievements of science and civilizations. They have tried black magic and astrology. They have fought wars, made slaves, committed suicide. They have sought solace and strength in worship of kings, demons, nature, or powers beyond nature.

One side of this problem comes out in a revealing phrase from Ernie Pyle, the news correspondent who got closest to the soldiers during the Second World War. In the men who faced death day in and day out he discovered an *"almost desperate reluctance to give up the future."* Many a man can verify that experience. In moments when death was near there came that yearning to live, to see home again, to rejoin family, to share the future. Here is the testimony that life is good — or we would not long for more of it — but that death constantly frustrates life.

In the story of *Moby Dick,* Herman Melville says, " All men are born with halters around their necks." Here is the most inescapable fact of all human life: *we are headed for death.* It is more than a fact; it is a powerful symbol of the frustration that threatens the human spirit.

Frustration, not pain, is the great human enemy. People bear even intense pains heroically and buoyantly when they see some accomplishment coming out of them. Plenty of evidence shows that people often prefer a life in which pain contributes some zest of accomplishment to a life of comfortable boredom.

But pain that is futile, that shows no doorway toward attainment, grinds down the human spirit. Uselessness, failure, defeat are more than we can stand. And *death* can mean all of these. Every human society has its customs and theories by which it tries to absorb the sting of death. But no society ever quite succeeds.

Often, of course, we manage to avoid thinking of death. Or we figure that "everybody does it," so naturally we'll be able to manage it when the time comes. Yet that doesn't solve the problem. For the frustrations of life come to a head in this powerful symbol. If we are destined simply to be wiped out, what is the point in our achievements? And if mankind is doomed to extinction, what is the point in the whole human story?

The *second side* of the problem goes still deeper. There is one experience far worse than "the almost desperate reluctance to give up the future." We might call it a "desperate reluctance to *face* the future."

The unusual person who is dominated by that experience is a likely candidate for a breakdown or suicide. But most people have flashes of this reluctance. It comes out in many ways.

Some morning, for instance, you wake up with an uneasy feeling. It's a beautiful day and you can't figure out what is the trouble. Then you remember. This is the day you have to get a tooth filled, or explain to the boss why you made a mistake, or tell an employee that his work is unsatisfactory, or borrow some money to meet a bill. The unpleasant expectation colors the whole day. But you live with it, get the experience over, and cheer up. So far, no great harm is done.

But life as a whole has something of that aura of dread about the future. In a healthy personality this foreboding is a subdued element, but psychologists from Freud's time until today have kept discovering it in people who don't want to admit they have it.

Such fear of the future is not just morbid imagination. After all, the world is frightening. Its evil and insecurity threaten human life constantly.

How can a sane person be comfortably " adjusted " to life in the twentieth century? We have fought wars on the big scale. We have seen tyrants who grasped after power and crushed their enemies with fiendish glee. We know all about torture and slaughter, hatred and crazed ambitions. We have invented new words (like " genocide ") to cover these activities.

Yet the events are not entirely new. Human history tells a lot about vicious deeds. Life always has its frightening side. It's not good to let these threats haunt us, but it's better to see them than to try to hide them.

Some people tell us, of course, that these troubles come from only a few big operators. But that is not true. Parents and adolescents and children can stage a little tyranny in the family. It all goes on within conventional rules, so that the neighbors seldom call the police. The weapons rarely (as in the comic strips) include the rolling pin. More often they are hot-tempered remarks, poses of moral authority, outbursts of tears, the playing out of the martyr's part, the control of expenditures.

Most of us are good at blaming other people for these problems in human relations. Husbands blame wives. Republicans and Democrats blame each other. We all blame the Russians.

Often, too, we blame ourselves. Every amateur psychologist — and that apparently includes most people nowadays — likes to diagnose " guilt complexes." What the amateur psychologists often forget is that some guilt complexes arise out of real guilt. Then the complex cannot be whisked away by giving it a label. Part of all human experience is recognition of the difference between what we are and what we ought to be.

We have been trying to locate a problem. We have found, in the midst of the goodness of life, certain deep difficulties. We have seen the threat of *death,* which makes us reluctant " to give up the future," and the threats of *life,* which make us fear facing the future. *Death* shows us our mortal incompleteness; it prods us into the brave attempt to relate ourselves to something that stretches beyond us and our human horizons. *Life* shows us discontents with our society and ourselves; it drives us to ask for healing of our human sickness.

The Urgency to Decide

Nobody decides to be born. Few people decide to die. But everybody has to decide what he is going to make of the problem of living and dying. Everybody has to do something about " the difference between things as they are and as they ought to be."

Notice that this difference has its good side. Without it there would be no aspiration, no effort, no attainment. It stirs mankind to great adventures. Because of it men are not vegetables but historical beings. And just because they are historical beings, they must try to discern where they are going, what they will make of life, how they will reckon with death.

One way to do this is to think seriously about human history and come to a set of reasoned conclusions that are called a " philosophy of history." Or we can — since the whole process is a long and difficult one — take over the philosophy of history that someone else has worked out.

The more common way is to leave the ponderings about history for the eggheads and get on with the practical business of living. There is a lot to be said for this way, since history seldom waits for us to understand it thoroughly. But notice that normal people do not simply side-step the great questions about history. Events force them to make some picture of their relation to their family, their nation, and the whole human story. They operate with some notion of what they may expect from the march of affairs. They have some conviction of the role they may play as the future keeps dawning, some attitude toward death. All this belongs to an *unconscious* philosophy of history.

The best-known example of a *conscious* philosophy of history is found in the Communist movement. Here is a clear set of dogmas about history. The philosophy predicts the future confidently. It fits all the facts, or alleged facts, into the system.

If most Americans are less dogmatic than the Communists, they have an advantage. They can be more flexible, more ready to adjust ideas to changing facts. But some Americans have just as dogmatic beliefs about history as the Communists. They "know" that God has a special destiny for the white race, or that success is the reward for being good, or that people with unconventional political beliefs are a threat to the world's progress. The fact that these doctrines are part of an unconscious philosophy of history is no advantage; it only helps people fool themselves.

It is time to summarize. If we list the main ideas so far (with slight changes in the order), we get something like this:
  1. Living requires venturing beyond our full understanding.
  2. Therefore we seek and rely upon certain clues.
  3. The great problem of human history is that
     — life with all its human illnesses drives us to seek healing.
     — death with its power of frustration drives us to relate ourselves to something larger.

4. Some response to history is inevitable. We want our response to be as intelligent as possible.

5. But the response is never just a matter of investigating the evidence. It has a deeply personal quality, depending upon what history has done to us.

6. The Christian finds the decisive clue to be the career of Jesus Christ.

The Testimony

A clue is never an isolated fact. It is the fact that shows the significance of many other facts. The person who discovers that an event is a clue moves quickly from it to a connected account of how many things fit together.

Hence, to recognize Jesus Christ as the clue to human history is not just to concentrate on Jesus. The Christian moves from faith in Christ to a testimony about the whole nature of God's dealings with men in life and in death.

To think through this testimony is the business of the rest of this book. To outline it in five statements is convenient now.

1. Christian faith testifies to the reality of God.

That testimony often leads to an argument. Sometimes it becomes an argument as to whether there is " a man upstairs," a sort of General who runs the show from headquarters but now and then steps in to settle something in the front lines. People tot up the evidence to support or refute the claim. Then they decide whether to believe in God.

All this has something, but not much, to do with belief in God. To believe in God is to testify that life is not just " a bad joke " or " a dirty trick," as some people have said recently. It is to say that we live in a world of purpose, a world where words like *reverence, fidelity,* and *love* are not nonsense. If the goal of life is only to keep some muscles and reflexes asserting themselves for a while, it is hard to see that it matters.

Belief in God is confidence that our spirits are related to a greater Spirit, to whom we respond with decisions that matter.

2. Christian faith testifies that God is eternal.

Some religions tell stories of the birth of gods. Less often we hear of the death of the gods. But Christianity — with most of the great religions — says that God is eternal.

At a minimum this means that God did not once upon a time get born — or happen on the scene and take over the job of being God. He will not someday resign or die.

But eternity means still more. It is not enough to think of God by adding years to years and centuries to centuries until we get so bewildered that we stop counting and say " forever." (After all, what do years and centuries mean before and after there is the solar system that measures off these periods?) Eternity means that God doesn't grow up, struggle through adolescence, strive to attain maturity, fight off senescence. He is not some cosmic nervous system. It does not make much sense to say that he is today ten years older than he was ten revolutions of the earth ago. No, eternity means more than a long, long, ever-so-long time.

3. Christian faith testifies that the eternal God is concerned with history.

Here many religions, which have been agreeing so far, stop. They say that it would be undignified of God to get involved in anything so common as a material world. Since he is un-changing, they say, he cannot condescend to get interested in a world where things corrupt and decay.

Such beliefs have tremendous consequences. The human story becomes a monotonous repetition. History is " just one damned thing after another " — to use a slang phrase with ab-solute seriousness. The way to find God is to get away from this Godforsaken world, to seek a mystical escape from history.

Christianity, however, inherits from Judaism an utterly different, dynamic sense of history. Change, which may mean decay, can also be creative. The eternal God himself is dynamic life. If we would seek him, we had better not run away from human responsibilities. He comes to us in the midst of struggle and adventure. History, though it has its dangers and frustrations, is alive with opportunity.

4. *Christian faith testifies to God's decisive activity in Christ.*

If Jesus Christ is *the clue* to God's ways with men, he leaves many riddles unsolved. Christian faith does not claim that history is a vast detective story that can be figured out from this one clue. The story is too intricate for anybody to put together and explain. If we want to know why Columbus got to America in 1492 or why the atomic bomb was produced in 1945, the Bible won't give us much help. The professional historians can give us some. For the rest, we'll have to stay ignorant.

It is in a different way that God gives us a clue in Christ. Try a comparison. The daily experience of family life gives a kind of understanding that a lonesome scholar cannot get from reading a thousand textbooks on the sociology of the family. Similarly Christian faith testifies that Christ, grasping a human life, gives an insight that no lonely study can win.

Our conventional chronology divides history into years B.C. and A.D. Is this only a slick trick on the skeptic who even if he writes an attack upon Christianity must date it "Anno Domini " (in the year of our Lord)? Or does it mean what it testifies — that God has done a crucial deed to conquer futility and death and our deepest discontents with ourselves? The only answer lies in the continuous test of history — the history we explore in the adventures of living.

5. Christian faith testifies that God's eternal power is not exhausted by history.

Without the power of the Creator God there would be no human life or history. Within history Christians recognize God's continued activity. (As we shall see later, it is often not the expected activity.) But history never shows the *full* power of God.

Almost everybody, Christian or not, at least halfway believes that last sentence. Notice why. Unless we grant that every successful tyranny deserves its victories — and who wants to admit that? — we are committed to an alternative. We are saying that we judge history by standards more important than historical success. As long as we see in history wrongs to be righted and wounds to be healed, we are testifying that we glimpse a standard of judgment that outlasts the struggles of history. This standard is not just the result of our whims or choices; it outlasts us too. The standard has, at the least, the power of truth.

So much is half the Christian testimony about the power of God that reaches out past our history. Then the testimony goes on: God's power can complete our little lives, heal our illnesses, bring eternal victory out of the tragedies of history.

There, then, is the Christian testimony — in five sentences with a skimpy explanation of each. Some of the holes will be filled in later chapters.

But first we must recognize that most of the world is saying, *Why should anybody believe this?*

The answer does not lie in piling up enough evidence to establish point 1, then gathering enough more to put over point 2, and so on. It's a quite different process. *This total testimony* is one way by which men live, meet their world, understand themselves and their relation to God. Inspect it as a whole. See whether it is ready to acknowledge all the factual data anyone can produce. See whether it grasps your loyalty and makes you testify too. See whether it makes the competing beliefs, by which many people live, look less honest, less powerful. If not, you *should not* believe this testimony. If so, you *will* believe it.

Those who do believe it find that the many substitute faiths dodge some aspect of life and history. The next chapter will look at some of the common substitutes. We need not beat the bushes to find them; they jump at us every day. By understanding them we can see the Christian testimony more clearly. Then Chapter 4 and the rest will go farther in examining the message of Christian faith.

SOME COMMON DODGES

Something in all of us resists the Christian faith. Something fights back, struggles not to be conquered, tries one way after another to avoid this disturbing religion.

Maybe we don't admit this. Maybe we hide it from ourselves. Sometimes we discover the fact only when we look at the elaborate hocus-pocus our world has worked out to dodge the problems of living and dying.

To talk about "some dodges" is not to talk scornfully about the people who believe them. Decent people accept and use these ideas. The Christian probably uses them too. He calls them "dodges" because he detects himself trying them whenever — and that's pretty often — he wants to escape his own declared faith. Now and then, however, he catches up with himself. Or he finds that God has caught up with him. And he realizes that he has been trying to escape a real decision.

By analyzing five of the most common dodges, we can understand ourselves better. We can also understand more clearly the Christian testimony. Often it gets hopelessly mixed up with the dodges. If we shake it loose, it may surprise us.

1. Up Know-how, Down God

A college student was sharing his troubles with a friend. He had plenty. He mentioned the draft, his uncertain career, a test he had flunked, and his unresponsive girl friend. Then, coming to a climax, he blurted out, " Sometimes I even wonder whether the world is getting any better."

The listener suggested that his friend was not the first who had ever wondered that. Somehow the idea shocked the student. " But," he answered, " if I didn't think the world was getting better, I would lose my faith."

He meant, strangely, that he would lose his Christian faith. But the New Testament, with all its confident rejoicing, frequently suggests that history will get worse before it gets better. It prepares Christians for suffering and persecution as dramatically as it announces the triumphs of God.

Nowadays, however, changing fashions have brought a " new look." People — often idealistic people — have said: " We're tired of talk about God's doings. We'd rather do things ourselves. We don't need otherworldliness, because we have the know-how to accomplish what we want."

Bertrand Russell announced that a hundred and fifty years of science had changed the world more than eighty thousand years of religion. He had some impressive evidence. The marvels of the machine age affect every hour of life.

The Church saw all this and wondered. Was its ancient message challenged? In that case, said some, " if you can't lick 'em, join 'em." They tried on the new look. They said, " When we talk about God's great power, we mean the wonderful improvement that is going on in the world each generation." Actually that is *not* what the Church had originally meant, but it sounded persuasive. The old faith dressed up in

the new one. God became so connected with historical progress that — as the college student found — when progress became doubtful, faith in God got shaky.

The fallacy in all this is not too hard to spot. Look, for instance, at these five examples of hopeful reasoning:

1. The TV images on the old set are blurred. But the new
models will show bigger pictures — and in color.

2. There are too many auto accidents. But next year's cars
will have better brakes and we'll have fewer wrecks.

3. Disease has always threatened life and made people in-
secure. But medical science has conquered some diseases. Soon
it will conquer more and make life secure.

4. The old wife is tiresome. But she can be traded for a new
model. It gets easier all the time. (Or, if you prefer, contracep-
tives make it easier to fool around with other women.)

5. The old self is a pretty grim one. But the new books tell
how to remodel it. They give the know-how for winning
friends, getting peace of mind, and living confidently.

Example No. 1 is not fallacious. It is a reasonable expectation
of technological progress. Our world shows so many examples
like No. 1 that people get in the habit of its style of thinking.
They unconsciously apply it to other examples, like Nos. 2–5.
They fail to notice that such cases involve quite different issues
from No. 1.

The trouble is that the progress of history solves some problems and makes others. Know-how gets misused. Swift planes
help friendships flourish around the world — and deliver de-
struction. Hitler finds a Goebbels (Ph.D. in psychology) to
manipulate and destroy people faster than more honorable psychologists can help them.

One famous man who got fooled on this issue was the
Frenchman Auguste Comte. He rightly saw that some people
use their hope of the next world to avoid improving this world.
So he predicted that the human race, by shaking off its hope of

immortality, would gain a " scrupulous respect for life " in this world.

His argument convinced many people. But is there anyone left who asserts that the twentieth century has shown more respect for life than the Middle Ages? or that the one great political movement that officially denies immortality (Communism) reveres life more than the rest of the world?

What has gone wrong? Working for social improvement was no mistake. The boner was putting history in God's place.

Maybe that last phrase sounds funny. But some men — a few of the French revolutionaries — actually addressed their prayers to history. More commonly, of course, people go on praying occasionally to " Our Father, who art in heaven," while really they count on history and the new models.

Then comes the letdown. As the grandiose promises of progress fail us, some say it's all a hoax. A few, it seems, even want things to go wrong so they can say, " I told you so."

But a Christian works to improve the world. His faith reminds him that the living God is active in history. He knows that " time won't stand still," that " you can't turn the clock back." (Those phrases, incidentally, have a Christian ancestry. Many great religions completely reject them.)

So the Christian expects change. He knows that history brings *new opportunities* and *new problems*. He'll use know-how because he worships God. That's entirely different from worshiping know-how.

2. Our Gang

Only a crazy man — like some crazy men who have become dictators of vast countries — thinks that history reaches its climax in himself. Most of us know that we are pretty small potatoes in the face of the problems of our own time, to say nothing of all history.

But what we do not claim for ourselves we may claim for " our gang." It's exhilarating to be part of a great group. That thrill belongs in human life. We find it in family, clubs, and nations.

But loyalty to our gang makes people do funny things. During wartime they rally their morale by singing, " There'll always be an England." Of course, there won't *always* be an England. And, though it may sound subversive, there won't *always* be a U.S.A.

One great industrial concern has its own anthem, in which the employees are supposed to sing:

> " We will toast a name that lives forever,
>   Hail to the IBM."

But one minute's thought about the meaning of *always* or *forever* is enough to set things straight. The chances are that patriots and industrialists know this.

Probably, too, most of the singers of sentimental college and fraternity loyalty songs are not really fooled. The claims of such songs usually involve only a fairly innocent blasphemy and a mild self-deception.

Sometimes, however, the matter goes deeper. A group or a nation announces that it really answers men's deepest problems and has a right to their total loyalty.

An American teacher and a Soviet diplomat met in Finland and got to talking about literature. They discussed a few prominent writers who had impressed both Americans and Russians. They wondered what peculiar skill these writers had. The American, Daniel Aaron, suggested one answer: that a writer in any part of the world had to be aware of the tragedy of modern life. To this the Russian replied with a perfectly straight face, " There is no tragedy in the Soviet Union."

Since then the party line has done some flip-flops and everybody is sure there was tragedy back in Stalin's time. But the diplomat's absurdity grew out of the Communist faith. Man's incompleteness and his discontents, he had to believe, were overcome in the Soviet system.

The world is full of berserk faiths that try to make a nation or race or social group divine. The Old Testament prophets had a rough phrase for this sort of thing. They spoke of forsaking God and whoring after false gods. Maybe that language should be revived today.

But before we throw the language around too loosely we'd better ask whether it applies to ourselves. If someone asks point-blank, we know that God is not the same as the American way of life or the era of economic security or the cozy family life of genteel white people. But these various temporary products of history, which deserve some respect, get a strong hold on us. We are likely to take them as the clues to history and to worship at their shrines.

3. A Gigantic Conspiracy

The two views we have looked at have not said much about death. Conceivably this might have been an oversight. But such is not likely. In fact there are signs that the ignoring of death, far from being an oversight, is a gigantic conspiracy. More than likely, we are among the conspirators.

Sometimes our whole civilization shouts at us: " Be happy! If you're dissatisfied, try a new gimmick — a new deodorant, dancing lessons, an escape movie on an extra-large screen, a seductive perfume, the auto that will impress the neighbors. As for death, forget it. Who wants ' pie in the sky, by and by ' when there's such a big pie to slice right here? "

The giveaway that shows the hollowness of this attitude is its very feverishness. It was done somewhat better by Epicurus, the ancient Greek. He taught that we should simply accept life's moderate pleasures and avoid its pains. The wise man relaxes in his garden and ignores the world's mad scrambling. As for death, it is simply the end of personal existence. With utter clarity he reasoned: When you are dead, you obviously cannot be hurt. Then why worry about death when you are alive?

Somehow that reasoning, for all its logical force, has seldom been convincing. A candid modern epicurean has said that the worse the world gets, the more reason there is to "eat, drink, and be merry." But, he adds, "The trouble is that I just don't feel like eating or drinking."

Possibly this man is the exception. Possibly most people today are adjusting to life and not worrying about death. Possibly rationality has overcome age-old concerns and has made death a simple fact instead of the powerful symbol of human frustration. But many evidences show that *the modern world is as morbidly preoccupied with death as any past age*. Consider a few examples.

Example 1. The Korean armistice provided for the exchange of bodies of the war dead. Some four thousand corpses were gathered by the Communists and returned to the United Nations command. Stretcher-bearers prepared the decomposing bodies for shipment home. One soldier, sweating in the repulsive work, asked, "Why don't they just let them be?" The officer in charge answered: "It's for the folks back home. Even if there's nothing left but a few bones, they have the right to them."

Why this concern with mangled flesh in a land where so many people supposedly accept Christian beliefs? Has some spiritual sickness so enfeebled us that the shipping of corpses is a consolation?

Example 2. Modern funeral customs make a desperate effort to hide the meaning of death. Friends who call on the bereaved are expected to gaze at the corpse and make pleasant comments about its looks. Cosmetic art dares death to peek through the mask its technique has contrived. When pastor or family prefer a funeral with no public display of the body, the mortician sometimes shows resentment; he has been deprived of the chance to advertize his skill in concealing death.

The profound meaning of the words " dust to dust " gets almost lost at the burial. The simple wood casket, which for ages helped Christians lay their dead in the grave with dignity, is out of style. Decorated bronze tries to veil mortality, for the bronze has been guaranteed in full-color ads " never " to leak. People forget that *never* is a long, long time. Take the word seriously and you get a vision of some future age when our solar system is reduced to cosmic dust; presumably there will fly about in space a few million bronze coffins, still not leaking.

Long ago Augustine wrote with pungent sarcasm: " If a costly burial does any good to a wicked man, a squalid burial, or none at all, may harm the godly." But such realism gets swamped in today's barbarous funeral customs. A vast industry tries to cajole us. The embalmer — probably as good a Christian as any other man, though it is hard to see any Christian reason for embalming — is a conspirator. And the rest of us share in the conspiracy. For our culture is so frightened of death that even in expressing Christian sympathy we feel compelled to help people forget death rather than face it courageously. We have to compromise with the futile solace of the social code or be inhuman.

Example 3. Even the Communists, who are supposed to have an answer for everything, give away their deep anxiety about death. Viewing religion as an opiate, they presumably laugh at the Old Testament Hebrews who, though reconciled to death, feared lest they have no male heirs, lest the family or tribe or name " be blotted out," lest remembrance be " cut off." But that threat persists in industrial Communist society. We read of traitors executed and buried in *unmarked graves,* their biographies cut out of the encyclopedias. Rationally, a materialist philosophy can conceive of nothing harmful to a dead man. But even there physical death becomes a powerfully symbolic blow at the worth of life.

Examples 4, 5, 6. . . . The squeamishness about death peeks through its disguises here, there, and yonder. Doctors say that many people avoid taking free chest X-rays for fear they might get frightening news. A specialist reports that even physicians are irrationally reluctant to take electrocardiograms because they might indicate heart trouble. Medical education suffers because enlightened people, presumably unworried by death, don't want their corpses dissected. The middle-aged person, reading a death notice, catches his mind swiftly comparing the age of the deceased with his own.

Thus death remains the most vivid symbol of the threat to all that matters. In superstitious ancient Egypt a ruler could direct the economy of an empire to building a pyramid supposed to stamp his fame on history and guarantee his future life. By contrast an American philanthropist has said, " The ownership of a fine library is the swiftest and surest way to immortality." No doubt the shift is an improvement, but it hardly solves the problem.

Shakespeare's Hamlet asks the profound question about death. Returning to Denmark from exile, he happens on the gravedigger who throws up the skull of Yorick, the court jester of Hamlet's boyhood. Hamlet feels the shock of mortality. What has this crumbling skull to do with the live person he had loved? From Yorick his thoughts move to the great men of the past. Can it be that imperious Caesar, who once held the world in awe, has become a lump of common clay that some man may use to patch his house wall? This is no mere conjecturing about chemical changes. Hamlet is asking about the worth of life — for a Caesar, a friend, or himself.

Imaginative writers sometimes try to picture the last human being on earth. They suggest the loneliness and futility of the solitary man who must ask whether his dying gasp is the end of the human story. Is this too fantastic to think about? In a way, each of us is concerned with exactly that problem. Does all the glory and tragedy of history lead up to one last death rattle? When all good and bad efforts are put in the equation, do they cancel out and give the answer of zero? Does the whole human enterprise lead to *nothing?*

This is the threatening question that society makes its silly gestures to squelch. Every day's living is affected by the deep securities and insecurities coming out of our struggle to dodge or lick that question.

4. An Endurance Contest

Often the human spirit refuses to believe in death. Notice that a majority of human societies have made some claim for life after death. Notice also the deep despair about death in some societies (like the ancient Babylonian) where no such belief is convincing. Here is evidence of the power of death's threat. But the wide diversity of beliefs about future life warns against leaping to conclusions.

Later (in Chapter 6) we shall look more closely at the Christian belief in eternal life. For the present we need to notice that *all beliefs that put the major emphasis on survival after death are dodges of our main problem.*

When we look at the New Testament message, we often miss one important fact. *The Pharisees* (who were the majority party among Jewish religious leaders) *already believed in life after death.* They did not need Jesus to tell them about that.

Certainly it was no mere belief in more life after this one

that transformed defeated disciples into a conquering Church. Christian faith proclaimed a victory — yes. But the victory was not just life after death.

At this point you may want to ask: " Why get excited about technicalities? Maybe some of these beliefs in survival are not exactly Christian. But shouldn't we be happy for everybody who believes in a future life? Then we can add to that whatever else the Christian teaching has to say."

The trouble with that question is that when we dig into the subject we find that belief in a future life may be no reason at all to shout. For instance, in the days when the Christian religion got started, men were hailing Epicurus (whom we looked at a few pages ago) as " savior." The reason was that he had removed their fear of a future life. Now they could settle down to enjoy this one.

Or come to 1886 when the British poet Swinburne wrote:

> " From too much love of living,
>   From hope and fear set free,
> We thank with brief thanksgiving
>   Whatever gods may be
> That no life lives forever,
> That dead men rise up never;
> That even the weariest river
>   Winds somewhere safe to sea."

That is probably not our typical mood. But something in us responds to it. Now and then the skeptic pokes fun by asking Christians whether they won't get tired of playing harps in heaven after the first thousand years. He doesn't understand Christianity, but he understands futility. Death is the great symbolic fact that reminds us of our incompleteness and the futility of many of our efforts. But to remove the fact is not enough, if incompleteness and futility remain.

5. Bridey Murphy, Spiritualism, and Assorted Guesses

Every few years someone raises a commotion by announcing that he has made contact with another world or another age. One notorious example is the Bridey Murphy ruckus. A Colorado woman, put in a trance by an amateur hypnotist in 1954, told of her previous existence in Ireland in the 1800's. When she proved able to talk in an Irish brogue about persons and places she could never have seen in this life, people got interested. Hundreds of thousands bought books and read newspapers about her or got recordings of her voice. A reporter, scrounging around in Ireland, found support for some parts of the story and threw doubt on others.

Then after a year and a half of arguments, the riddle broke. The mystifying Colorado woman in her childhood had lived in Chicago across the street from an Irish woman whose maiden name had been Bridie (*almost* Bridey) Murphy. The various details that came out in hypnosis matched forgotten childhood memories. The Bridey Murphy fans relapsed into quiet — waiting for the next fad to come along.

The name for this belief in repeated existence is *reincarnation*. The theory is about twenty-five centuries old. It has persisted among millions of Hindus and Buddhists. But they have not been happy about the prospects. The idea of repeating life, round and round through endless incarnations, turns out to be as discouraging as the endurance contest. The Hindu and Buddhist religions, therefore, offer a discipline to dissolve individual personality and stop the ceaseless round.

So the Bridey Murphy story is interesting mainly for what it shows about the eagerness of people to get excited about flimsy evidence. In between the occasional spectacular announcements many people are continuously visiting "spiritualists " or " mediums." These practitioners try to bring messages from departed relatives or at least some assurance that the spirits of the dead still live somewhere.

Investigation has exposed some of the quacks who work their hoaxes to get money out of gullible people. More recently some psychologists have tried to conduct honest research into psychic phenomena. Such research can inspect the available data with scientific method rather than with the prejudices of partisans on both sides. Like all scientific inquiry, it must simply work with the evidence and formulate whatever hypotheses are most adequate. The rest of us can only wait to see what it turns up.

But the hypotheses of psychic research do not have very much to do with the Christian confidence. It is pathetic to see how some people stake their whole conviction upon bits of pseudoscientific evidence. And the anxiety with which some people look for solace in the operations of a medium is as far from Christian trust as any atheism.

For Christian faith is always more than ferreting out new data. Honest faith will, of course, look at any evidence. But new facts are, at best, possible clues to understanding the mystery of our history and the ways of God with men. And the choice of the master clue is still a deeply personal choice.

Yet even though Christ be our clue, we hanker after some of the dodges of this chapter — and some more. Though we see through them, we like them. They are easier than facing the majesty of a holy God.

If, however, we recognize these dodges, we are ready to examine in more detail the Christian testimony about God's Lordship over life (Chapter 4) and death (Chapter 5.)

4

God Acts — but How?

Some people believe in a " sleeping, snoring God." Others believe in a God who acts. That was Martin Luther's way of stating the contrast.

Thomas Carlyle, the gloomy Scotsman, could not share Luther's belief in a God who acts. A friend once told the old man that he could believe only in a God who *does* something. The weary Carlyle replied with a cry of pain, *" He does nothing! "*

From Genesis to Revelation the God of the Bible *does things*. He is an active, vibrantly dynamic God. But *what does he do?* We can examine some answers in terms of four " case studies " from modern life and from Scripture.

Case Study 1: " Lord of Hosts "

Go back just a few years to the time of the Second World War. In the Pacific Ocean the greatest sea fight of all history is going on — the Battle for Leyte Gulf. In a bold American initiative General MacArthur has just waded ashore in his long-promised return to the Philippines. But the Japanese fleet is assaulting the American armada of more than seven hundred ships. The attack moves brilliantly. The Japanese tactics have decoyed the main American fighting vessels out of position and (as Hanson Baldwin later tells the story) Admiral

Kurita has "victory in his grasp."

Then a sudden counterattack by a few small American torpedo boats throws confusion into the opposing forces. Events turn dramatically. The Americans, pushing their gain, sink or damage most of the great Japanese ships. That once mighty navy will never make a major stand again.

An American admiral comments on the unexpected reversal of the battle. He says it can "be attributed to our successful smoke screen, our torpedo counterattack . . . and the definite partiality of Almighty God."

That statement leads some people to say amen and others to snicker. Before looking at it more closely, move back through history to a time before 1000 B.C.

The Israelites are invading Canaan. The nomads, coming from the desert, lack the military skills and weapons of the Canaanites. The enemy under General Sisera masses big armies and hundreds of terrifying iron chariots. The two sides join battle. An unexpected storm bogs down Sisera's chariots and the Israelite foot soldiers win. They celebrate with a song of triumph and thanksgiving.

How did they gain the unexpected victory? According to their report, "The Lord routed Sisera and all his chariots and all his army." Their God, Yahweh (or Jehovah), came amid thunder and lightning from his home in the south to deliver the decisive blow at the crucial hour. He caused the heavens to drop water. True, the Israelite soldiers fought with valor. But they did not fight alone.

"From heaven fought the stars,
     from their courses they fought against Sisera."

The victory showed the "partiality of Almighty God." (You can read the story and the song of triumph in Judg., chs. 4; 5.)

This sort of thing happened a number of times in Old Testament history. The people continued to praise God for their victories. They called him "the Lord of Hosts," "the Lord mighty in battle."

But sometimes the Israelites got licked. What then? Maybe God had forgotten them, some thought. Or maybe they had traveled too far out of his territory and should shift allegiance to local gods. Sometimes they tried just that. After the next battle they might switch back or they might stick with the new gods, depending on how things went.

Clearly there is a good deal lacking in this reasoning. But before looking at the defects, notice one element of insight. It sees that the great decisions of history are not so completely our doing as we like to think. When we win a battle, we can respond in three moods:

1. We can be grateful.
2. We can take the credit ourselves.
3. We can figure luck was with us that time.

It is not clear that moods 2 and 3 are more mature than mood 1 — whether in Palestine or at Leyte Gulf. Similarly, when our foreign policy doesn't produce the miracles we expect, we are not always wise to figure that some traitor sold out or that a Secretary of State blundered. History is not just the product of our manipulations. The Hebrews saw this better than many of our politicians and pundits.

But now consider the defects in this level of reasoning. *Difficulty 1* is that the Israelites did not understand the "laws of nature." They attributed to God specific activities that we explain otherwise.

We should not be too supercilious at this point. Our best scientists are not entirely sure what a law of nature is and are even less sure why there should be any nature or any laws of nature. And the Israelites, who were not stupid, knew about the regularity of natural processes — about steady sequences of " seedtime and harvest, cold and heat, summer and winter, day and night " (Gen. 8:22). They knew, long before Jesus reminded them, that God's sun rises " on the evil and on the good " and his rain falls alike " on the just and on the unjust " (Matt. 5:45).

Yet it remains true that modern science has influenced us powerfully. Our experience has impressed us, more than theirs had impressed them, with the possibility of understanding even the abnormal hurricane or earthquake in terms of normal natural processes.

Difficulty 2 is more religious in nature. The case study shows a belief that God is on one side, trying to defeat its enemies. The enemies, of course, take a different view. If Leyte Gulf showed God's partiality, what about Pearl Harbor?

The belt buckles in the old German army said, *" Gott mit uns."* Some of those buckles lingered in Hitler's army. But then every nation says, " God with us." Those that try not to believe in God say " historical destiny " or " the future of civilization."

It took Israel a long time — and it is taking the world a longer time — to learn that the great battle between God and his enemies is not a battle between nations. Some of these international battles are important to halt vicious tyrannies. But the great battle goes on *inside every nation* and *inside every person*. God judges and condemns the evil in *us* as well as that in our enemies.

Difficulty 3 arises when we ask what really happened in this case study. Presumably God took charge of a situation to strike a spectacular blow against some human power that was in the wrong. But more realistically we have to say that wrong never gets really smashed that way. It may get some of its weapons crushed, some of its striking power taken away. But evil smashed is evil still. Evil disarmed is less harmful than evil armed — but it is just as evil. If God's purpose is to remove evil, that purpose must find another way.

To think through this difficulty, however, requires the rest of the case studies.

Case Study 2: " The Wages of Sin "

Begin with one of the seething Asiatic areas where a revolution has thrown out Western government — perhaps Indo-China where French troops and American money took a beating not so long ago. Someone says: " This was bound to happen. The long evils of colonialism produced this revolution. The white man should have known it was coming."

Someone else answers: " But what about those tyrants who took over? Are the Communists any better than the imperialists they drove out? "

Now move back to the time when Isaiah is prophesying in Jerusalem. Earlier prophets in the north have told their people that the rottenness of national life is bound to bring God's judgment. Confirming the prophecies, the Assyrians have overthrown the Northern Kingdom (Israel) and now threaten the Southern Kingdom (Judah).

Isaiah faces a puzzling problem. Can this military threat be God's judgment? Can a just God punish even a sinful people with the vicious Assyrians?

In ch. 10, Isaiah reasons his way through this situation. His ideas come out in vivid, impassioned poetry. If you break up the poetry and examine the logic, you find something like these four steps:

1. *Yes,* Assyria is " the rod of [God's] anger." Judah has

sinned and deserves this punishment.

2. But *no,* Assyria does not aim to serve God. In haughty pride she thinks only of conquest and plunder.

3. Hence Assyria's conquests will not last. God will take care of her, as he is now taking care of Judah.

4. But the message for Judah is to repent and recognize a deserved punishment. Then a "remnant" of Judah will return to God.

There are other ways to express the same ideas. A proverb says, " The mills of the gods grind slowly, but they grind exceedingly fine." A paraphrase of Isaiah's theme might run: " Sin will catch up with you. For a long time you may get away with something, but God is not mocked. The wages of sin is death. And don't complain that death comes via another sinner. He'll get his wages too."

This " prophetic interpretation of history," whatever its problems, represents a triumph of realism that is still beyond most people. Nations today hate to recognize that many of their troubles are judgments on their sins. Nevertheless it makes sense to say (echoing Isaiah) that the wrongs of the West often lead to the successes of the Communists, but (still echoing Isaiah) that the Communists are defying God and preparing their own downfall.

Abraham Lincoln expressed eloquently this prophetic understanding in his Second Inaugural Address. For while he made his prayer that war might soon end, he recognized that it was the consequence of men's sin:

" Fondly do we hope — fervently do we pray — that this mighty scourge of war may speedily pass away. Yet, if God wills that it continue until all the wealth piled up by the bondman's two hundred and fifty years of unrequited toil shall be sunk, and until every drop of blood drawn with the lash shall be paid by another drawn with the sword, as was said three thousand years ago, so still it must be said, ' The judgments of the Lord are true and righteous altogether.' "

With all its profundity, however, this prophetic interpretation of history is not adequate. In the first place, it leaves too many loose ends. It finds God always a step behind evil; and while he is catching up, too many people suffer unjustly. Pretty soon — in fact, right within the Bible — it provokes people to say: " Wait a minute. *Some* disasters are the just payment for sin. But what about the least guilty people who sometimes get hit the hardest? Not *all* the sufferings of history are the wages of evil."

In the second place this prophetic teaching easily gets turned around. Examine these two statements:

1. Sin brings punishment as a consequence.
2. Mr. A is having troubles; he must have sinned. Mr. B is pretty well off; he must have pleased God.

Statement 2 is not the *logical* consequence of statement 1. Mr. A's troubles may be due to other causes than sin; and Mr. B's prosperity (like the Assyrian's) may be building him up for a letdown. But the people who are thriving generally manage to slip quickly from 1 to 2.

So in the Bible itself prosperous people misused the prophetic understanding of history to congratulate themselves. And today many political speeches, editorials, and articles in national news magazines take the same line. They say: " Look at our peace and prosperity. Doesn't this show that we have lived right? Our initiative and effort are bringing this reward. God must be mighty pleased with us. But look at those rascals in other countries. Their cities got chewed up in war and their crops won't feed their people. They could learn a lot from us. They'd better, if they want to get out of their difficulties. God is just!"

The prophets answered this sort of reasoning in language that, if it were repeated here, would be considered quite ungracious in a religious book.

Jesus finally declared the incompleteness — not the entire falsity — of this view of history. Someone told him that Pilate, the governor, had killed some Galileans who were making religious offerings. Jesus announced that the slain men did not suffer because they were worse sinners than other men. But giving the prophetic teaching its due, he said to those about him, "Unless you repent you will all likewise perish" (Luke 13:3). Sin produces suffering, but the victims are not always the worst sinners.

Case Study 3: "Wounded for Our Transgressions"

Look at a scene in American history more than a century ago. A group of Negro slaves are toiling in the fields under the blazing sun. They have been kidnaped from their homes, dragged to this nation, put to work for whatever rewards their masters choose to give them.

When evening finally brings relief from heat and work, you hear them singing: "Nobody knows the trouble I see." "Were you there when they crucified my Lord?" "It's me, it's me, it's me, O Lord, standin' in the need of prayer." No one can explain why, in God's world, these people were made slaves. But out of their suffering they are creating songs of faith that become one of the glories of America.

Now move back once again to more ancient times — to a group of exiles in the sixth century B.C. They too are slaves of their conquerors — Jews in Babylonia. Out of their despair they ask, "How shall we sing the Lord's song in a foreign land?" (Ps. 137:4).

But one of them learns to sing it as it has not been sung before. His poems are now included in the book of Isaiah (chs. 40 to 55). He sings of the glory and majesty of God. This Exile proclaims that even the greatest nations are like drops of water before the Almighty God, yet that even the least of people are his concern.

Then he thinks specifically of the suffering of his own people. He sees in it judgment, for they have sinned. But that does not satisfy him. He is convinced that they have received more than enough punishment, that God has forgiven them, that God offers them renewal. So his song is of comfort — and to this day Americans hear it every year at Christmas time, in the words of the King James translation and the music of Handel's *Messiah:* "Comfort ye, comfort ye my people, saith your God."

Still the poet ponders the suffering. He does not explain it, but he catches a vision of opportunity. It is possible, he says, to bear the sorrows of others, to accept pain in innocence and thereby help the guilty find healing. Again his words live in the memories of people today:

> " He is despised and rejected of men; a man of
>   sorrows, and acquainted with grief. . . .
> Surely he hath borne our griefs, and carried
>   our sorrows. . . .
> But he was wounded for our transgressions, he was
>   bruised for our iniquities: the chastisement
>   of our peace was upon him; and with his stripes
>   we are healed.
> All we like sheep have gone astray; we have turned

> every one to his own way; and the Lord hath
> laid on him the iniquity of us all." (Isa. 53:3-6.)

The poet's words with their haunting beauty leave a puzzle.
The ideas those words convey are never quite brought together. The writer tells of the mighty God, Lord of the ends
of the universe, the Sovereign who gives to the nations their
destinies, even though most of the nations do not know Him.
And he tells of God's Servant, whose suffering brings healing
and redemption to men in the midst of this vast drama of
history. It is not quite clear how the two themes fit together.
We can only ponder them both — and wonder.

Case Study 4: "The Power of God for Salvation"

This time we cannot shift from a modern to an ancient
story. This case study is unique. For the Christian who wonders how God acts, this is *the clue.*

Focus your view on a hill outside ancient Jerusalem. There
a man hangs on a cross. He is, we are told, a man who has
gone about doing good. He has taught God's will and has
healed the sick. He has gathered a few followers — not that
they are much in evidence at this stage of the story. He has
excited the people by promising a marvelous act of God asserting his sovereignty (or, in New Testament language, his Kingdom). He has worried the leaders of the people, who say he
is a subversive. They have engineered a trial with trumped-up
accusations. Now they are killing him.

Next shift your focus to some events of the following years.
A group of Jews are scurrying across land and sea, gathering
little communities of people, arousing them with news of
God's wonderful acts. Some of these bold men are the old followers of the crucified man, whom they knew as Jesus of

Nazareth. The most influential of them (Paul) never knew this Nazarene. But all of them are saying that the one God of the universe, who through the ages has done so many mighty deeds, has now done the mightiest work of all.

Why did they say that? Anybody could see that the enemies of Jesus had killed him. By most men's logic that left just two choices. *Either:*

1. God was against Jesus; *or*
2. God took a beating from evil.

But a different logic offered a different choice. Through the empire went the gospel ("good news") that God had won a victory on that hill. Now, said the witnesses, we have seen "the power of God for salvation" (Rom. 1:16). "In Christ," went the message, "God was reconciling the world to himself" (II Cor. 5:19). God "disarmed" the agents of evil and "made a public example of them, triumphing over them in him" (Col. 2:15).

But was the example "public"? The crucifixion, of course, was plainly visible. It was, in our modern language, "publicly verifiable." But the *victory* was not obvious to every detached observer. Most people saw no triumph at all. Even those who were most sure of it talked much of the *mystery* of what God had done.

To understand what they were getting at, look at what they reported — not all of it, but just these three points:

1. God won a glorious victory on the cross.
2. God confirmed that victory in the resurrection of Christ.
3. God continued the victory by sending his Holy Spirit upon men.

The scoffers looked at that report and called it a hoax. They could answer it point by point:

1. A victory on the cross? What a cover-up! Everybody knows that an execution is a defeat.

2. A resurrection? It's a fake. You can't prove it.

3. The Holy Spirit? Purely subjective. A lot of emotionalism.

How do you referee an argument like that? Neither side can convince the other. There's no *proof* to satisfy the "objective bystander."

It is easy, if you are determined enough, to call the Christian testimony subjective, since it depends on personal response. But — remember Chapter 1 — *every* conception of history depends on personal response to what happens. One bitter skeptic has said, "Jesus trusted in God, and God let him down." Another man, who started as a bitter skeptic, ended by saying, "For the word of the cross is folly to those who are perishing, but to us who are being saved it is the power of God" (I Cor. 1:18). Why such different accounts of the same event? Because the cross did nothing marvelous to the first skeptic, whereas it brought a saving power to the transformed skeptic, Paul.

Certainly there is nothing subjective about certain activities that followed the cross. Men who had been weak and uncertain stood up with amazing confidence before angry mobs. They prayed for those who lynched them. They shook the assurance of their legal judges and converted their jailers. Nobody was twisting the arms of these Christians to make them keep up the pose. No brainwashers were forcing them to testify to something they didn't believe. They were convinced of *victory*.

Basic to the whole story is a new idea of *how God acts*. The old versions of God's acts in the affairs of nations had sunk into men's consciousness. The poems of the Suffering Servant had sunk in. The impact of Jesus upon those who knew him had sunk in. And out of it all came the testimony that God won a victory in those events on Golgotha.

It is vastly unlike the victory of Leyte Gulf and most other victories we talk about. Most of the world has now heard about it, but the world still doesn't know what to believe. To understand it requires that we look for the *hidden* activity of God. It requires that we look past the obvious commotions of history to recognize *what God is doing to people* in those events. God, acting in Christ, brought — and still brings — faith and healing and transformation to people.

And now we see why it is not mere verbal magic to call that obvious defeat a hidden victory. It would have been no such victory if Jesus' followers had boldly marched up the hill, seized him from the Roman soldiers, and spirited him away. Or if Jesus in Gethsemane the night before had made a dash for freedom. Or if on the cross he had turned hatred on his tormentors, instead of saying, "Father, forgive them." These would have been victories for his foes.

But the foes could not conquer the love of God, which men came to recognize in Jesus Christ. And empires with soldiers and lions and more crosses could not conquer the Spirit let loose in the world.

We have looked at four case studies. No case tells the whole story. No case rubs out those that went before. Each transforms those before it. Now we can think more clearly about how God acts.

The Freedom of God

Providence is the word used to describe God's activity. Newspapermen and historians, in writing their accounts of human affairs, rarely use the word. They have good reasons for leaving it out:

1. The non-Christian does not want the word, because he probably does not believe in Providence.

2. The Christian, knowing the *hidden* quality of God's activity, will not rashly explain that activity.

Yet Providence firmly belongs in Christian faith — if we can get rid of one misconception that sometimes makes this whole belief sound foolish. We get a picture of two worlds: this world and the other world (somewhere upstairs). We can understand this world in terms of normal causal principles. But from time to time a hand reaches down from the other world (maybe through a hidden trap door in our ceiling) and interrupts the causal process with some marvelous deed. Then the hand goes back, and normal cause and effect continues.

But that misconception is neither realistic nor Christian. It turns history into a mechanical process and makes God a grandiose manipulator.

The Christian account says, by contrast, that every day of the world's history is full of wonder. For every day a *free God* is dealing with his *free creatures*. In this relationship both God and man act purposively and responsibly. Hence throughout all life, not just in rare events, men find the beauty and love and holiness of divinity.

You can, of course, reject this belief in freedom. You can try to figure out history entirely in terms of economic and geographic and psychological causation. You can say (with the great French astronomer Laplace) that long before there was any solar system or human race the laws of nature and the distribution of matter in a primeval nebula determined everything that would ever happen on this earth. The Battle for Leyte Gulf was settled then. All future human struggles, however uncertain they now look, were settled then. So was your career — your marriage, your vocation, the fact that you are at this moment reading this book and agreeing or disagreeing with it.

In the Christian belief, however, each day is really new. Granted, the history of yesterday is part of today; but today is not just more of yesterday. This day calls for *new* decisions, presents *new* opportunities, demands *new* responses.

God's freedom and men's freedom keep meeting, sometimes clashing. Men and nations resist and defy God. They prefer to run things their own way. They ask for trouble — and get it.

Constantly God calls us to make decisions. He does not make the decisions for us, because he is no string puller manipulating his puppets. Each day he addresses us: "Choose you this day whom you will serve." Often the choices oppose God. But God in his freedom has ways of dealing with us. There is a "partiality of God."

The Partiality of God

The British historian Herbert Butterfield says in his book *Christianity and History:* "I am unable to see how a man can find the hand of God in secular history, unless he has first found that he has an assurance of it in his personal experience." Most Christians agree. This means that Christian thought works from the inside out. The Christian, responding to God's activity in Christ, can look for signs of similar activity in the great expanse of history. This method leads to three statements about God's dealings with men.

1. *Providence is dynamic and revolutionary.*
The "Song of Mary" in The Gospel According to Luke (ch. 1:51 f.) says of God:

> "He has scattered the proud in the imagination of
>   their hearts,
>   he has put down the mighty from their thrones,
>   and exalted those of low degree."

This is a rather startling description of the way God acts. It runs counter to some common assumptions about how God helps those who help themselves. But notice how consistently the Bible asserts this theme. (*a*) The Old Testament prophets repeatedly announce that God's judgment falls especially upon the haughty. (*b*) In Luke the quoted words refer specifically to God's gift of Christ. (*c*) Jesus' Beatitudes (Matt. 5:3-11) announce God's revolutionary blessing upon the poor in spirit, the meek, the persecuted. (*d*) The cross of Christ — understood as apparent defeat but genuine victory — is the clinching testimony to this exaltation of the lowly.

Now we must ask, Does this teaching really fit history? The answer must be a careful one. Obviously the Bible is not a book on "How to Win Empires and Influence Nations." If God's work is characteristically a hidden work, it won't show through history so that we cannot miss it. But what faith sees clearly in the Biblical story may appear — somewhat dimmer and vaguer, to be sure — in general history. We may find that belief in Providence helps us understand the daily news.

Thus Providence means that history cannot be frozen. The future keeps coming. And the future brings changes that threaten especially the proud and self-satisfied. Perhaps God today is not doing his most powerful work through the men who think they pull the strings of the American economy and government. Perhaps he is preparing to exalt the Negroes of America or South Africa, the hungry and illiterate folk of China and India. Perhaps the complacent and unjust privilege of powerful groups today is ripe for judgment.

All this does not mean that the Christian supports every revolution that comes forward with a few weapons and a slogan. Sometimes greedy men try to overthrow haughty tyrants in order that they may themselves become haughty tyrants. But because the Christian believes in God's kind of revolution, he will look for signs of creativity in human revolutions.

2. *Providence turns men's acts to unexpected results.*

God calls for men's willing service. But the Bible often asserts that God is sovereign even when men ignore or defy him. He lets men have their freedom, but he remains Lord.

Again the cross of Christ is the striking evidence. Here men are at their worst. Yet God so handles their deeds that today Christians sing, " In the cross of Christ I glory." We need not conclude that God endorses wickedness or indifference. But he can make even " the wrath of men " to praise him (Ps. 76:10).

This power of God has its wider parallels. Arnold Toynbee in his famous ten-volume *Study of History* has a fascinating phrase — " the irony of history." The great efforts of history, he says, usually have quite unintended results. For instance, the Roman emperors built great systems of roads and swept the pirates off the seas — all for the purpose of preserving their empire. Actually, says Toynbee, their purpose soon failed. The most lasting result of their whole effort was to help the travels of an obscure citizen they did not even know — Paul, who carried the story of Christ from the outposts of the empire to its capital city.

It is Toynbee's thesis that the most enduring thing any empire does is to contribute — quite unintentionally — to the growth of a great religion. Perhaps this is an exaggeration. Providence often works through less obvious ways than the spread of religion. But, if the cross of Christ and the history of Israel are clues, the Christian will look for the hidden activity of God in unexpected places.

This does not mean that the Christian hastily concludes that every flourishing movement is somehow doing God's will. Some people, seeing the power of a movement, get a sort of mystical intuition that it must be God's destined plan. They talk knowingly about a " wave of the future." This sort of reasoning led some churchmen to support Hitler and others to hail Communist gains. Christianity cannot agree that military or political success is any guarantee of divine approval. But it can look to God to use even man's defiance for His purposes. And the Christian, seeking to serve his God, will always seek possibilities of redeeming evil situations.

3. *Providence seeks to save people.*

In the midst of all the fireworks of history the main providential activity continues. Everybody gets excited about the lesser struggles. The great struggle still matters most.

On Golgotha, God did not strike down Pilate and the Sanhedrin. He has ways of dealing with the powerful, we have seen. But his most *crucial* act (to use a word that comes from " crux " or " cross ") was of a different sort.

It is usually that way. Martin Luther once observed: " If the Turk destroys cities, country and people, and ruins churches, we think a great injury has been done Christendom. Then we complain, and urge kings and princes to war. But when faith perishes, love grows cold, God's Word is neglected, and all manner of sin flourishes, then no one thinks of fighting."

Today everyone knows about the great struggle between East and West. We worry when things look bad, cheer up when tension relaxes. But a far greater struggle is going on: the struggle of God against sin. This battle crosses all the other battle lines. It rages in East and in West, in all our institutions and in our inmost selves.

To recognize it helps us to put the more obvious struggles in perspective. We will not lose interest in them. We can carry on the great battle only as we are faithful in the midst of the lesser battles. But we will not think, if we understand the Christian faith, that history's problems are solved when we become stronger than our national enemies; or that God's most characteristic activity is his blows against our enemies.

God would win us to himself. This is the goal of Providence. He will not overrule our freedom. He did not deny freedom to Judas, even to prolong the life of Jesus. He will not force us to submit. He has acted in history to win a victory and to offer us a victory.

That victory, wrought in the midst of our human history, reaches out to eternity. To see its meaning we must look to man's destiny in eternity.

DESTINY IN ETERNITY

We usually think of doubt and faith as opposites. The doubter is called an agnostic. Unlike the Christian, who believes in God, and the atheist, who denies God, the agnostic keeps saying, " I don't know." He seems to lack the courage of his convictions, because he lacks the convictions.

Sometimes that picture is true. But sometimes it is dead wrong. Everyone is an agnostic on some questions. In fact, one sign of Christian maturity is the ability to say, "I don't know."

"It's Not What You Know . . . "

Imagine two men on a three-day fishing trip. In the evening they get into a conversation.

SMITH: What's your wife doing tonight?
JONES: I don't know. She thought she might invite a few friends in. But she said she might go to a movie.
SMITH: Doesn't that bother you — not knowing what she's doing?
JONES: I hadn't thought of it. It didn't seem to bother her. She enjoys an occasional evening with her friends — same as I enjoy fishing. As a matter of fact, she said that if she could

get tickets, she'd phone your wife and ask her to go to a concert.

SMITH: That was nice of her. But my wife is busy. I know what she's doing every night I'm away.

JONES: You do?

SMITH: Sure. Last night she had a committee meeting for the women's club. Tonight my mother is having her in for dinner. Tomorrow night she's promised to work on her household budget. She doesn't know it, but I've arranged for Charlie Brown to phone and ask for me — just to find out for sure that she is at home.

JONES: What's the idea of all that?

SMITH: Well, these women get lonely when we're away, and you don't know when they might step out on us. I don't believe in taking any chances.

JONES: Well, I just hadn't worried about that.

SMITH: You mean you don't know where your wife was last night?

JONES: That's right.

SMITH: And tonight?

JONES: Check.

SMITH: And tomorrow night?

JONES: Look. She's got a mind. She can decide for herself.

SMITH: That's the trouble. They *do* decide for themselves. How can you trust your wife if you don't know what she's up to?

JONES: Are you sure you trust yours?

SMITH: You bet I do. I know where she is every night.

JONES: Oh. . .

You don't have to be a psychoanalyst to recognize that Smith does *not* trust his wife. Because he has all the anxieties of distrust, he has to be shown that she is not up to mischief.

Smith is likely to go on worrying for a long time, because there is a basic fallacy in his whole method. All his scheming **may** convince him that his wife is behaving herself, but it cannot convince him that she is *trustworthy*. And whether he realizes it or not, that is what he really wants to know.

Jones, who trusts his wife, doesn't have to know what she is doing every minute. He has confidence in her.

If the two men transfer these same attitudes into religion, they will come to conclusions something like these:

SMITH: I want my preacher to give me definite answers to my questions. I want to know how God runs this show. Why shouldn't I find out what heaven and hell are like? How can I live right if I don't know the rules for the Last Judgment? How can I believe in God if the preacher won't answer my questions?

JONES: I guess there are a lot of things we can't know and don't need to know. Naturally we'll think it all out as far as we can. But when we can't go any farther, why worry? After all, if things are in God's hands, they are safer than if they depend on our doping them out.

If you ask why, in the midst of many uncertainties, the Christian believes in God, the answer is in the whole nature of the Christian faith. (That's why there are twelve books in this series, including one on just that subject.)

But if the answer must be put in a paragraph, a common slang phrase will help. "It's not what you know, it's who you know." When the string puller uses that phrase, he means that the right connections will get you farther than honest efforts. But the phrase hides a profundity that the sloganeers never suspect. It's not what he knows about the future that makes the Christian confident; it's the God he knows.

So, he testifies, the whole quality of human life is a *re-*

sponse to God and God's world. When he tries to get away from God, he cannot; responsibility (response-ability) continues. When he trusts God, he finds himself freed of illusions, able to face facts squarely, close to the realities of existence. To clinch and transform it all, when he sees Christ he finds himself responding to God in the midst of men. And though this Christian resists, God will not let him go. Sooner or later he finds that he is glad that God won't let him go.

This kind of faith, with its accompanying ignorance, is involved in all Christian thinking. It becomes most obvious when we ask about the destination of life.

Destination vs. End of the Line

Most trips have a destination. You get into the auto, train, or plane with the intention of getting somewhere. Even if you just go for a walk, you aim to get home. When the trip ends, you have arrived.

Occasionally a trip has no destination. Accidentally you get on the wrong bus. If no one alerts you, you just keep going. After a while you come to the end of the line. The bus goes no farther, but you haven't arrived. After getting over the bewilderment, you start traveling again. You want the *end* of your trip to be your *destination*.

Human life is a trip — an extended trip, which includes many side trips along the way. Here arises the great issue. Does life itself have a destination, or do you just come to the end of the line? Two answers are possible:

1. Although every person's life is full of goals that he chooses, life as such, by its very nature, has no destination.

2. Life has a purpose, and the many goals along the way are helpful or harmful as they lead toward or away from the great destination.

Obviously life has an "end of the line" — death. Beyond

that point there are no roads, no rail tracks, no visible mark-
ers. Equally obviously, the end of the line is not a destination.
No one lives for the sake of dying. The children's stories end,
" And they lived happily ever after." Actually that ending is
a double lie. First, the word " happily " hides all the troubles
" they " must have had. Second, " ever after " really means
" until they died." We don't want to say that — in children's
or old people's stories. A story dares not come out *nowhere*.
In stories as in life everyone asks for the " end of the line " to
become a " destination."

The same issue arises for history. Men will not live on this
planet forever. Astronomers tell us that the sun will end human life — if human ingenuity doesn't do so first. That means
that human history comes to the end of the line with an unin-
habitable earth. Again, two answers are possible:

1. History, though crowded with purposes twisting in one
direction or swerving in another, finally comes to the end of
the line and nothingness.

2. History has a purpose, because a divine Destiny gives it
a destination.

Our answer is more important than we like to think. It is
not just a conjecture about something remote. For a future
goal is never merely future. It is part of our present awareness. It sets the direction of life now.

Suppose, for instance, that you are on the train to Washington. Some of the externals of the trip — the schedule, the curves
in the tracks, the temperature of the cars — are the same for
everybody on the train, whatever his purpose. And no one else
on the train knows why you are making the trip, unless you
choose to tell. But *to you* it makes all the difference in the
world whether you are going there to marry your bride or to
testify to a Congressional committee about your criminal activities. Maybe you get so interested in a pinochle game that you

momentarily forget the purpose of your trip. But soon you remember, and that purpose colors your whole trip. The *future* goal is a *present* part of your consciousness and behavior.

Similarly every person's final purpose influences his whole life. Side interests (like the pinochle game or much bigger things) are interesting enough that people temporarily forget where they are going in the long run. Thus many a person who sees no purpose to life will, out of natural vitality or generosity, do worth-while things. And many who believe in a high purpose will, out of natural cussedness, do evil things along the way. (We all have our generosity and our cussedness.) But when a genuine sense of destiny — or of futility — governs a life, the difference is momentous.

That momentous difference is the subject of Christian faith. For this faith testifies that this human story, whatever it looks like, is no wild melee of forces competing brutally until they all fade out at the end. God will transform the end of the line into a destination.

In Christian vocabulary, one word for this belief is "eschatology." The word (all five syllables) first hit newspaper headlines during the Second Assembly of the World Council of Churches at Evanston in 1954. But the *meaning* of the word has always been part of Christian life. The word (from Greek) means "a belief about the end." It is the doctrine that under God the end is a destination.

So Christian faith declares that, whatever powers control life, God's power is *final*. He has the *ultimate* resources, the *conclusive* voice. In the *last* analysis he is Lord. In the *end* it is God who matters.

Notice how those five words in italics all have a double meaning. They can refer simply to the end in a series (e.g., the *last* man in line). Or they can refer to the deepest truth of the present (e.g., the *last* analysis, which usually means a present analysis that gets at the truth).

That double meaning is important. It tells us that the God who will outlast history is God now. The goal of it all is part of life right now. History drives toward a destination that gives the dynamic struggle its zest and meaning now.

Not everyone agrees, of course. But notice that eschatology, generally speaking, is not some weird possession of the curious people called Christians. *Practically everyone has some sort of eschatology.* That is, normal human beings have some notion of the purpose of it all, some idea of an outcome that affects the way they live now. Look at some examples (which may remind you of the " dodges " in Chapter 3):

. . . The Marxist believes in a destiny (called " the dialectic of history ") that drives society through a series of revolutions to the victory of the proletariat. Eventually, then, the state will wither away and everyone will work for the good of all. The Marxist is glad to hurry the process along, but he can afford to be patient when necessary, since his goal is certain to come. He needs no hope beyond earthly history. When the source of evil (private property) is done away, heaven on earth will arrive.

. . . The Epicurean — remember him? — believes that history is going no place. Deep futility hangs over life and makes any great effort useless. In the absence of a destination, the thing to do is make the best of the present. As for the future, why worry? You won't be around for it.

. . . Somebody else — he used to be rather common, but is harder to find now — says very conscientiously that this generation finds its purpose in making life better for the next. The next will do its bit for the one after it; that one will strive for the sake of the next; . . . until the last one, which will die out.

. . . Another person — perhaps he calls himself an "existentialist" — says that this unfriendly world dooms all achievements. The one thing man can do is assert his freedom. There's no point in heroics for the sake of social improvement; each of us is a lone individual. But in each moment of decision a man makes his destiny. So long as he asserts himself, he is somebody. Then it all fades out.

. . . A nationalist, who might live in Russia or China or America, believes that his destiny is his country's. Perhaps he hopes that his country will always be right, but in any case he shouts, "Right or wrong, my country." Perhaps that problem never comes up, since right is by definition the advantage of the country. Anyone who threatens the nationalistic creed is a subversive. The most dangerous are those "do-gooders" who talk about internationalism, read books by foreigners, hoist United Nations flags, or even suggest that God is not a——— (fill in Russian, Chinese, American, or whatever fits).

. . . Then there's the person who can't be bothered with it all. He's meeting the payments on the mortgage and improving the house a bit. He has a retirement pension, social security, and a few war bonds. He wishes the television didn't have so much alarming news, but he doesn't see what he can do about it. As for death, medical science makes that less uncomfortable all the time.

There are other current eschatologies, better and worse than these. The point is that you don't decide whether or not to have an eschatology. You decide which one is yours.

"Thy Kingdom Come . . . . Thine Is the Kingdom"

Do you ever think carefully about the Lord's Prayer as you say it? (It's been done.) If so, you find yourself in some eschatological meditations. Near the beginning you say, " Thy kingdom *come*." This is a petition. It expresses yearning for something unrealized. It asks that something happen.

At the end you say, " Thine *is* the kingdom, and the power, and the glory." That is not a petition but an acknowledgment. It testifies to a reality.

What is this " kingdom " that you have been talking about all your life? Have you been inconsistent — now asking for it, now acknowledging that it is a fact? Or would it be better to forget the whole subject, now that kingdoms are going out of style?

Before deciding, take a look at the New Testament. The message of Jesus centers upon the Kingdom of God (as Mark and Luke call it) or the Kingdom of Heaven (Matthew's way of saying the same thing). Obviously Jesus is not talking about a political domain located, say, between Palestine and Egypt or between Palestine and the Big Dipper. We come closer if, whenever we say " God's Kingdom," we think " God's reign."

But that phrase " God's reign " poses a big question. Is there ever a time when God does not reign? He is the Creator and Lord of the universe. He is Alpha and Omega (Greek equivalent for " A " and " Z," meaning beginning and end). Jesus did not have to announce that God reigns. The Jews believed that. In prayer they addressed God as " king of the world."

So to pray, " Thine is the kingdom," is to acknowledge that God is sovereign. Maybe that looks like a harmless bit of pious language. Actually — as many a big operator from Nero to Hitler has discovered — it is as potent a sentence as any human being can utter. It says that whatever sovereignty

the U.S.A.	claims over	land and people
family, church, or club	claims over	its members
an individual	claims over	his own life

—all these are lawful and good only when they do not claim too much. God's reign is the real reign, the reign that dwarfs all the rest and that lasts forever—"as it was in the beginning, is now, and ever shall be."

Yet that is certainly not the whole story. Because there are other factors in the situation, the Christian prays, "Thy kingdom come."

God reigns, yes. But the world constantly defies God's reign. Only the techniques vary. The blatant tactic is to say, for example:

. . . "I don't like you, God. If I believe in you, I'm supposed to believe that men of all races are one in Christ. I won't take that, even from God."

The subtle tactic modifies the language:

. . . "I like you, God. Whatever the radicals say, I know you made my race superior to these others. You belong in my corner."

The twentieth century has seen plenty of both approaches. In fact each of us runs his own rebellion against God. Not that we get away with it. God's sovereignty means that our very rebellions against him only enslave us to political tyranny, money, or other fearsome gods of our own time. Yet defiance continues.

Hence today as in Biblical times people recognize something incomplete in God's reign. They long for God to expose the impostors—the men and forces that claim a sovereignty that they have no right to assert. So, in the Lord's Prayer, Christians pray that God will bring men to serve the Kingdom that they now rebel against. They say, "Thy kingdom come."

Today, however, we do not say it exactly as the disciples did when Jesus *first* taught them the prayer. We say it as they did *after* they had witnessed the crucifixion, met their risen and living Lord, found the Holy Spirit invading their lives.

Thus the note of expectation joins with the note of triumph. God *has* invaded history. In Christ he has declared himself, asserted his sovereignty. He has done it, as God usually does things, in the way people did not expect. The majority did not notice it or were not convinced. But to those who responded in trust and confidence, God *did* expose the impostors and grant freedom from slavery.

In the Lord's Prayer, then, as in the whole Christian faith, there is this harmony of acknowledgement, anticipation, and realization:

acknowledgment — that God reigns from everlasting to everlasting;

anticipation — that God's glory will be made known throughout all creation;

realization — that faith has already seen God's reign invading human history in Christ.

It is sometimes said that Christians live "between the times." That is, they celebrate God's victorious deed *already done* in Christ. They *look forward,* longing for all heaven and earth to respond to the love and Lordship of God.

The excitement of living in such an age runs through the whole New Testament. Christians still find that excitement in life today.

Just What Do Christians Expect?

History "between the times" is an adventure. And adventurers need guidance. But no tourist agency will plan this trip, secure the tickets, and make the reservations.

Foolish curiosity asks for a road map of the future. Desperate anxiety demands the map. But maps are not available. It is a mark of maturity — we have already seen — to be able to say at the right time, "I don't know." Candid confession of ignorance is always better than pious bluff.

But it is only because he has a basic confidence that the Christian can admit ignorance without worry. In the absence of road maps he has the guidance of a *memory,* an *awareness,* and an *expectation.* He remembers what God has done, he is aware of what God is doing, and he confidently expects this God to continue his faithful activities.

So the Christian, sharing the ignorance of all men about the future, makes some reasoned guesses that overlap the reasoned guesses of people around him. But soon the reasoned guesses merge into his faith in God and God's ways of dealing with men. So the outlook shapes up something like this:

1. Through the ages God has led history into new situations with new problems and new opportunities. The Christian will continue to expect the unexpected. The atomic age opens new horizons and new perils. The coming of "one world" of communications and human relations demands new ways of living. As always, faith must pioneer.

2. The struggle between good and evil will continue. Evil will find new disguises. Good can expect new persecutions and new triumphs. Each day brings new demands for loyalty, new blessings for faith, new glimpses of God's activity.

3. When the story of earth is all told, the living God will continue to reign eternally.

That last statement is the one that raises the questions. The curious keep pressing for details. For the gullible, someone is always ready with an answer. Maybe he has been counting letters and numbers in the New Testament and has doped out the year of the great cataclysm. Maybe from the poetic imagery of the book of Revelation he has put together a picture of what life is like in a world after this one.

But the Christian will remember two examples of the restraint of Jesus. (1) Impatient with idle curiosity, Jesus said that only the Father knew the answer to some of these favorite questions of men (Matt. 24:36). (2) Jesus described the circumstances of life beyond death only in terms of parables.

We can learn a lesson here from the Christian memory. Imagine a news photographer at Golgotha. He would get his motion pictures and his sound track of the crowd and the lonely man dying on the cross. *He would not get a picture of God or evidence that God had done anything there.* Perhaps, compared with a Cinemascope extravaganza, his film would be unimpressive and disappointing. For the glory and the meaning of the event are not on the surface.

Imagine, then, a camera set to grind away automatically at the last chapter of human history. Whether focused on the last human activities or peering into the cosmos for signs of God, it might miss everything important. God's reign is not photographable. Most descriptions miss the point.

The Christian believes in eternal life, in a destination that is not a mere end, in a coming Kingdom of God. Of the details he is ignorant. But because of what God has done, he is confident that God will do more.

Now put together some fragments from various chapters of this book. We have seen how man is haunted by " the difference between things as they are and as they ought to be." History invites him to heroism in the service to God — heroism that can do great deeds. Yet history itself can never deliver him from its own frustrations. For though history completes some beginnings and rights some wrongs, it always leaves loose ends untied and brings new corruptions into its successes.

The Christian proclamation is that God overcomes the difference that history can never remove. *God completes the incompleteness of history. God meets*

history's weariness	*with*	*renewal,*
its sin	*with*	*redemption,*
its wounds	*with*	*healing,*
its death	*with*	*life,*
its frustration	*with*	*victory.*

His eternal power has streamed into history from the cross; that eternal power will outlast history.

That is not a promise that God will change what we have to what we would like. We have seen enough of his ways to avoid that trap of immature religion. But in the end we can be glad that the future is in his hands rather than ours.

6

OLD PHRASES THAT STILL SAY SOMETHING

This book, like all books, has been written before its author's death. The author, like all authors, has had no "contact man" in the world beyond to relay him tips on how things are shaping up. He cannot offer any "inside dope."

Some people think they can. A certain Richard Hull of Scotland, for instance, arranged to be buried upside down on his horse. He expected the world to be turned over at the Last Judgment, and he wanted to be ready to gallop.

Conjectures like that have made some of the old Christian phrases sound foolish. But most of those old phrases have deep meanings. It is possible to discover those meanings without being taken in by the weird speculations that often go with them.

Death and Resurrection

Many religions and philosophies teach that *life continues after death*. The Bible instead promises that *God will raise the dead*. The New Testament — though it uses a variety of phrases, as though to say that no one of them can be literally exact — most often talks of death and resurrection.

That is no accident. Nor is it, as some say, an immature Hebrew statement that we can replace with the more rational belief in a soul that never dies. If we look at the words — not for a blueprint but for an insight — we find them saying three things.

1. *Death is a major event.* We cannot dismiss it as unreal or insignificant. The Apostles' Creed says bluntly that Jesus Christ was " crucified, dead, and buried." It does not say that he " passed away " or " went to his heavenly home."

People have rightly admired the heroism of Socrates, who calmly faced death saying that his foes could not really hurt him. Here was magnificent courage. Some have said, " He is a greater spirit than Jesus of Nazareth, who approached death with the struggle in Gethsemane."

But the Bible does not recommend a casual, philosophic attitude toward death. For death is momentous. It is the hour at which our whole earthly record stands closed. Then we can no longer lightly say, " I'll make up for that tomorrow." The New Testament, with all its confident faith, acknowledges the seriousness of death when it says, " Greater love has no man than this, that a man lay down his life for his friends " (John 15:13).

2. *God raises the dead.* This is not the theory that we never die because we are just naturally indestructible. It is the blazing declaration that though it is our nature to die Christ has conquered sin and death.

Resurrection is God's miraculous work. It is as pure a miracle as the creation of personality — out of a few dollars' worth of chemical elements. (Notice that neither *miracle* is a violation of natural laws.) Hence it is appropriately called the " new creation."

Perhaps this is why John Calvin, who knew that many pagan philosophers have believed in some kind of life after death, nevertheless wrote: " But let us remember that no man will be truly persuaded of the future resurrection but he who is filled with admiration and ascribes to the power of God the glory that is due to it."

3. *The new creation is really new.* Jesus tells Nicodemus that unless a man is "born anew"—"born of the Spirit"—he cannot enter the Kingdom of God (John 3:3–8).

The New Testament is a song of triumph:

> "O death, where is thy victory?
> O death, where is thy sting?"

But notice why death has lost its sting. The next sentence explains that "the sting of death is sin" (I Cor. 15:55, 56). Eternal life, far from merely prolonging the old life, is the conquest of sin and death in new creation.

The Christian artist Rouault has made an engraving with the title "Arise, ye dead!" He shows skeletons coming up from the dark ground into a light that radiates from three distant crosses. At first glance the viewer wonders: Why these ghastly bones? Why this bizarre combination of a victorious smile on the jaws of a skull? Why not beautiful bodies instead of skeletons? Then he sees what Rouault is saying—that God does not neatly bypass death. Out of the grave itself, with its total threat to all hope, God calls forth new life.

One great question remains. When does all this happen? Occasionally in the New Testament it seems obvious: sometime after we die God raises us. But often it appears that this great event *has already taken place* in the Christian life. Faith brings eternal life into this life.

Just this is the Christian experience. Paul describes it: the person *dies* to sin, lets self-centered ambition be *crucified,* and *rises* with Christ into a new life of trust and love. (See Gal. 2:20 and Rom. 6:3, 4.) Hence Christians, facing their persecutors, could say; "We have no fear of death, because we have already done the dying that hurts and have found the glory beyond the pain."

For most of us, however, that statement would not be honest. We haven't got that far. Perhaps Paul best sums it up by saying, " I die every day! " (I Cor. 15:31). Death to sin is *past* in the decision to become a Christian; it is *future* in the resurrection beyond the grave; it is *present* in the continuous struggles of living. Hence many Christians agree with Sören Kierkegaard, who said that it is impossible to *be* a Christian; one can only *become* a Christian. In becoming Christian we are dying and rising.

Yet God works marvels even in this *becoming*. Not because death is trivial, but because so much of death and resurrection were already done, Francis of Assisi could end life with the words, " Welcome, Sister Death."

Body and Soul (or Cemetery and Heaven)

Children ask difficult questions about cemeteries. Maybe we all do, but children do it out loud. Grandmother has been sick, then has died. Someone tells the child that Grandmother has gone to God. But someday the child asks about the grave-yard. Is Grandmother in the cemetery or with God?

One answer is: Grandmother's body is in the grave, but her soul is with God. With luck that answer stops questions.

Someday, then, the child hears the Apostles' Creed: " I believe in . . . the resurrection *of the body*." His question usually brings the answer: " That really means the soul." Now and then someone insists that it really does mean the body. Maybe he opposes cremation, because he wants his body ready for God to raise in the Last Days — though why God should have more trouble with ashes than with decomposed flesh is not clear.

Pretty soon a nonsensical argument is under way. Notice how the New Testament dismisses these futile guesses:

1. The bickering Sadducees ask Jesus about the widow who remarries. (Just to be smart alecks, they give her seven successive husbands.) Who will be her husband in heaven? Jesus, who never avoids a sincere question, gives this one the brush-off. You can't answer questions about heaven in earthly terms, he tells them. You don't understand the power of God. (See Mark. 12:18–27.)

2. Someone presses Paul with a question about the bodies of those raised from the dead. The apostle, who always likes a good question, explodes, " You foolish man! " (I Cor. 15:36).

Some questions are just futile. Whenever we use words out of common experience to describe the works of an infinite God, the words don't quite fit. Literal answers to questions about life after death are mostly foolishness.

Once we realize this, we can go a step farther. An artist spreads pigments on a flat canvas to suggest not only dimensions of depth but hidden experiences of the human spirit. A musician uses vibrating strings from animal intestines to convey joy, humor, or grief. Words similarly have symbolic power. They may tell us more when we realize their inadequacies than when we think they give us literal truth.

When the early Christians said " resurrection of the body," they were not kidding themselves. They were not slow-witted people who had not thought of the question the child asks about the cemetery. They said clearly that "flesh and blood cannot inherit the kingdom of God." Decay of corpses was no problem for them. Yet they found reason to hang onto this idea of a body — a " spiritual body," they called it. (You can find all this discussed in I Cor., ch. 15.)

The New Testament could have used different language. All the educated people had heard the theory that at death the soul soars to heaven while the body goes to the grave. But that language did not click with the Jewish Christians who wrote the New Testament.

The Jews just never had believed that a person is a soul plus a body — a detachable combination temporarily hooked up. Today practically every psychologist agrees with the Jews on this issue. When we talk wisely of psychosomatic medicine or trace a person's disposition to the activity of his glands, we are doing (with more or less scientific precision) what the Biblical writers did intuitively. In Christian history, Augustine did the same thing when he said, in words that all our modern knowledge vindicates, "For the body is not an extraneous ornament or aid, but a part of man's very nature."

Some very "spiritually minded" people argued against this Christian belief. They quoted Plato's *Phaedo:* "Whence come wars, and fightings, and factions? whence but from the body and the lusts of the body? . . . And what is purification but the separation of the soul from the body?" For Christians this was an utter evasion. It meant unhealthy abhorrence of the body and blindness to the sins of the spirit.

So the Church hung onto its concern for a complete person, not for a soul plus a detachable body. It preached God's salvation of real people, not of mystic souls that might get absorbed in some divine soul. It taught God's concern for history, realizing that most history is connected with human bodies. So, at the risk of being misunderstood, it kept talking of a resurrection of the body — meaning not the chemical components of the body but the wholeness of the human being.

None of this tells us *literally* and *exactly* what is going to happen. Of course not. "O foolish man!" We cannot know. Christian faith, we have seen, talks of a new creation as miraculous as the first creation. The only basis for belief in it is trust in God. If that does not convince us, neither will any enticing preview of coming attractions.

The Last Judgment

Hollywood, with all its delight in spectacular "Biblical" films, has not yet done the Last Judgment. Why has it missed this opportunity for dazzling splashes of Technicolor on a screen big enough to show all heaven and earth? Perhaps because the scenario writers have not yet figured out the sex angle. Possibly because even Hollywood realizes that ultimate judgment cannot be put on a screen.

Painters and poets have sometimes tried. Now and then they have conveyed some hint of the portentous character of the Last Judgment. More often they have failed. Words and pictures are likely to become ludicrous. Then, instead of trembling at the Last Judgment, we make a wisecrack about Gabriel's horn or Peter's keys.

Yet we never quite escape the notion of the Last Judgment. We only conceal it. Then occasionally something jolts us to consciousness of what judgment is all about.

Arthur Miller's great play, *Death of a Salesman,* did that for some people. They met Willy Loman, the jolly good fellow who drifted through life convinced that to be "well liked" and have the right contacts was the way to success. They saw Willy live by his creed and teach it to his sons. They saw him carry his deception almost to the end, when it collapsed in the awful discovery that his business associates and his boys and even Willy Loman saw through the bluff.

The response to the play was startling. When it went to Europe, the newspapers there expressed amazement that America — the land of the success story — could produce a play about failure. In this country people wondered why this play fascinated its audiences as more glittering shows did not.

One day a newspaperman asked the author for his own opinion of the power of the play. Arthur Miller explained that his play dealt with a problem that concerns everyone. It is, he said, "the fear that one has lied to one's self over a period of years in relation to one's true identity and what one should be doing in the world. What the play does is to make the individual ask himself whether his rationalizations about himself are not leading him to an ultimate rendezvous with a dreadful reckoning."

That is what the doctrine of the Last Judgment is about. Life, of course, is full of judgments. Every day we try to impress the people judging us — and that includes everyone around us. We feel hurt that people disapprove. Or we gloat that we gain their approval. All the time we know how inadequate these judgments are. No one judges us with real accuracy. We even deceive and misjudge ourselves.

Still we have a deep recognition that to fool our friends and ourselves is no advantage. We are responsible before a truthful judgment.

Now forget all the trivial speculations you have heard about the Last Judgment and see what a powerful influence that Judgment is upon life *now:*

1. We know how to rate all our cheap successes when we think of the "ultimate rendezvous with a dreadful reckoning."

2. We quit asking anxiously, "What will folks think of me?" when we understand the importance of "what God thinks of me." We can take social disapproval, resist the desperate urgency to conform to the going patterns, when we acknowledge our responsibility before God.

The Last Judgment, it turns out, is not just something the other side of the grave. "And this is the judgment, that the

light has come into the world, and men loved darkness
rather than light, because their deeds were evil " (John 3:19).
The Last Judgment has been going on for a long time. Like
death and resurrection, it is part of life now.

Heaven and Hell

In the Middle Ages the poet Dante wrote a description of
heaven and hell. He laid out a cosmic geography, locating the
earth, Garden of Eden, Jerusalem, hell, sun, stars, the seven
heavens. He enlivened his terrifying descriptions of hell by
spotting some of his personal acquaintances at nasty locations
in the area. He described heaven too, but not so vividly as
hell.

Somehow writers never make the bliss of heaven quite so
impressive as the flames of hell. It has been reported, however, that the heat of hell has no terrors for the Eskimos, who
are more disturbed by a frigid hell. This information is
trivial, except that it shows the futility of some of our descriptions.

Imagination is a poet's privilege and does no harm, provided no one is misled. But some people are misled. In sober
gullibility they frame notions of heaven and hell that have
no basis in fact or reason, in Christian experience or faith.
They are simply foolish conjectures.

Often they are worse than foolish. They are subversive of
Christian faith. They have led such honest men as the phi-
losopher Spinoza to say that the Christian ethic is too cheap,
since it uses future reward as a bribe to entice men to behave
now. This criticism fits fairly some teachings, that say in effect, " If you will just stop being self-centered for a few more
years, you can enjoy self-centered delight forever." Such a
crafty plot for personal gain will never lead anyone into the
life of love.

A better lead comes from John 5:24, where Jesus says: "Truly, truly, I say to you, he who hears my word and believes him who sent me, has eternal life; he does not come into judgment, but has passed from death to life." To know God *is* eternal life. The peace of reconciliation and the exhilaration of courageous service are eternal life.

Is this all? No, it is not all. But it is the real thing. Ask the Christians whose confident faith guided them through Hitler's concentration camps. They can testify to the gifts God gave them there. They found eternal life. They might say, "This is *it,* but it is not *all.* This is eternal life invading time, our best clue to eternal life ahead."

All this may sound disappointing. If your appetite has been whetted by a Moslem picture of the marvelous foods and beautiful maidens in heaven (or an American advertiser's picture of the heaven money can buy), you may say: "If you are talking about heaven, I'm not sure I want it. It doesn't sound worth the struggle."

Exactly right! Something in all of us is dissatisfied with heaven. We have a continuing yen to feed the insatiable cravings of the self-centered ego.

And that helps us to know what hell is. To be offered love and to refuse it is hell. To disdain to trust the trustworthy is hell. Now and then (like Willy Loman) we recognize the utter emptiness and intense despair of hell. And something in the nature of human responsibility tells us that even death (like Willy's suicide) is a dodge that will not succeed. We can make a hell too secure to evade with a mere bullet or gas jet. Again this hell on earth is *it,* but not *all* of it. For no one can describe the agony of life with all pretenses gone, clinging to the misery of isolation rather than risking surrender to love.

Sooner or later someone always asks: Does punishment in hell go on forever? One ancient theologian taught that all rational creatures, including Satan, might eventually be saved. Another forgot his New Testament long enough to teach that one of the joys of heaven will be watching sinners (below in hell) get their due forever.

If we go to the gospel itself, we find two themes that must influence all Christian thought. First, the New Testament tells of the unconquerable love of God. Any Christian who sees the depth of God's mercy toward him will be in no hurry to deny that mercy to other sinners. But second, the New Testament tells of the urgency of decisions. It is not enough to keep saying, "There's always tomorrow to turn over a new leaf—if not in this life, then in the next." Some choices today rule out other choices tomorrow.

Farther than this the New Testament will not take us— unless we want to choose up sides and throw proof texts at each other. (There are some available for both sides.)

The Roman Catholic doctrine is clear. In February, 1955, the pope declared that really bad sinners suffer in hell forever. An omnipotent God *could* remit punishment, the pope granted; but, he said, God "never has granted it and never will do so." One can only ask, "How can he be so sure?"

But go back five paragraphs. If hell is "clinging to the misery of isolation rather than risking surrender to love," it is not a mechanical punishment for past crimes (like a spanking or a jail sentence). It is the choice of the sinner. Perhaps God eternally offers mercy to the sinner, but never *forces* the sinner to love. Whether punishment is eternal then depends on whether man chooses eternally to rebel. And who knows what that choice may be?

All these descriptions fall short, as any talk of eternity must. They are simply a fumbling attempt to show what the Christian gospel means for our thoughts of heaven and hell. Surely that is better than trying to smuggle a pagan heaven and hell into Christianity.

The Return of Christ

Talk of the Second Coming of Christ usually belongs to the curious sects who from time to time predict the end of the world and train their eyes upon the clouds. They have been mistaken too often in the past to be convincing today.

But those groups should not be allowed to do all the talking. Their mistake is to forget that the great acts of God are usually not the ones that register on the moving film and the sound track. (Recall Chapter 5.) If we get past this fallacy, we can see why the New Testament not only remembers Christ; it also expects him.

The first reason is that Christ returns whenever we welcome him. "Behold, I stand at the door and knock," he says. Every day he is coming; and he continues to come. The wisest attempt to define the boundaries of the Church is the old one, "Where Christ is, there the Church is."

The second reason is that the God of Christ always has more to do with us. In our lives and churches God's absence is all too impressive. Human history (as we have seen) needs God to transform its end into a destination. But the God whom Christians expect at the destination will not come as a stranger. He will be the same God who in Christ asserted his Kingdom and did his reconciling work. To believe in the return of Christ is, above all else, to believe that history at its destination faces the God who in Christ has already come.

"Now we see in a mirror dimly, but then face to face" (I Cor. 13:12). That sentence combines (1) the Christian confession of ignorance with (2) the Christian declaration of faith. We need to keep the two together. It is a fallacy to say either, "Because of our faith, we know all about the future"; or, "Because we don't know the future, we can't have faith."

Books belong to the *now;* they cannot get behind the dim mirror. But this is no real loss. To demand to know more than you can know is to force yourself into a logical dilemma: If you trust God, you need no details to give you confidence. If you do not trust God, you have no reason to believe the rest of the details. It's that simple.

GOD OF THE LIVING

Some years before the climactic days of his career, Winston Churchill said, " There never was a time when the hope of immortality and the disdain of earthly power and achievement were more necessary for the safety of the children of men."

To many people back in 1932 that was a curious statement. They answered it by saying: " No! If you want a better life, get your mind off other worlds and make your achievements here."

Yet as the twentieth century moved on into its fateful years of decision, Churchill's reasoning became more convincing. Over and over again, human safety, which is never a sure thing, depended on the courage of some who threw their lives into struggle because they found a greater issue than their own survival.

Possibly Churchill recalled those earlier words when he led his nation through the Battle of Britain. Certainly their spirit stuck with him. For looking back on the exultancy of that heroic Battle of Britain, he has said, " This was a time when it was equally good to live or die."

Life has moments like that. The dramatic power of a situation raises men far above their normal selves. In such a time of destiny they are ready for anything.

The trouble is that we cannot live a whole life on the basis of momentary exhilaration. The truth is that we are very human. Our moods vary from day to day. We are heroes and cowards, optimists and defeatists, adventurers and loafers. We never are sure which we shall be next week.

In this perplexity Christian faith tells us that despite our varying psychological states, we can constantly know the conviction of destiny. We don't have to count on our moods. We can count on God.

To live *today* is our immediate business. But today can never be entirely hemmed in between last midnight and next midnight. For today includes memories that stretch far backward and expectations that reach far forward. It includes beliefs about all of life, death, and destiny.

In this book we have been exploring these beliefs. Recall the path we have taken.

We started with some common questions about the ways of God with men in life and death.

We hunted for an answer by trying to find what God does to people in their history.

We found that what he did in Christ convinced some people that here was the clue to his ways with men.

We watched the clue develop into the Christian testimony. And we compared that testimony with some other beliefs that Christians try when they want to dodge God.

We examined the testimony about God's power in human history. We saw signs of his activities — though not the activities that just anyone might expect.

We examined the testimony that God is the eternal Lord over death, Author of the new creation.

We found in this whole Christian testimony the conviction that God offers the healing and completion that we cannot give our own lives and history.

Once again, then, look at the difference this testimony makes. Compare two sayings that show the opposite possibilities of the human adventure. The first comes from Paul: "For to me to live is Christ, and to die is gain" (Phil. 1:21). There is the confident faith of a man writing in the prison from which he was soon taken to his execution. The second is a phrase from a popular song — "tired of living and scared of dying." Those words — more bitter when we examine them than when we sing "Old Man River" — express despair.

Normally we do not choose either of these expressions as personal slogans. In fact, we make an art of living in the middle area, filling our days with enough activities that we need not face the naked issue. But even this middle area requires decisions. Inevitably, admitting it or not, we find our lives guided by those two radical possibilities. Either life is futile or we can do something.

But what can we do? The Christian testimony shows the way between two booby traps that catch almost everybody now and then.

Booby trap No. 1 is the illusion that we can accomplish almost everything. In personal life it is the notion that we can plan our children's lives or remake our marriage partners or scheme our way into happiness. In public affairs it is the chesty expectation that the right know-how, the right expenditures, the right alliances will settle the destinies of nations as we have planned.

But we are wiser to be more humble. Herbert Butterfield writes: "The hardest strokes of heaven fall in history upon those who imagine that they can control things in a sovereign manner, as though they were kings of the earth, playing Providence not only for themselves but for the far future." Against this grandiose pose the Christian testimony reminds us that other people have something to say about the course of events and that God has something to say to us all.

Booby trap No. 2 is the opposite illusion that we can do nothing. Its slogan is, "What's the use?" Its personal wail is: "I haven't a chance; ____ [the draft, the boss, my wife, my parents, my children] don't give me any breaks. I can't plan or control anything." Its public lament is: "Let's quit pouring money down the rathole. All we've done has been useless. If ____ [foreign countries, the public schools, juvenile delinquents] want to go to hell, let them go."

To the futilitarians the Christian testimony says that each day brings opportunities that a faithful boldness may grasp. If we cannot remake life or history, we can examine both and throw our weight into the important struggles.

So we can walk between the booby traps. God does not ask us to run the universe. He will do that. He asks us to serve him. Pascal once wrote: "We always behave as if we were called upon to make the truth triumph, whereas we are called upon only to struggle for it." If booby trap No. 1 tempts us to think that truth's triumph depends upon us, booby trap No. 2 tempts us to give up the struggle. Pascal's alternative is the faith that God, who can make the truth triumph, has a special place for our acts of loyal service.

In his Providence, history always offers opportunities, whatever our position. Note a few examples.

If public office (or democratic citizenship) be our role, God invites us to seek justice and peace, to serve the nation without worshiping it, to guide the body politic in ways of righteousness.

If prison be our role, God invites us to bring the gospel to prisoners and to our jailers — as did Paul in Caesar's prison and Dutch, German, and Norwegian prisoners in Hitler's prisons.

If parenthood be our role, God invites us to show our children
his gospel and give them the opportunity to choose loyalty.

If earning our daily bread be our role, God invites us to serve
mankind in work and to bring his love and his gospel into
the crowded ways of life.

When death is our role, God invites us to continue our trust
in him.

Thus life and death become opportunities for citizenship in
that Kingdom which has no end. This is no guarantee that
our acts are bound to succeed. Even loyal efforts may crash in
failure. But the God who transformed the cross into the sign
of victory can use failures. His hidden activity can bless and
redeem any loyal response to him.

For he is Lord of life and death. To know this, says John
Calvin, "means gratitude in prosperity, patience in adversity,
and a wonderful security respecting the future."

God calls men today. He calls them to a destiny in history
and in eternity. As Jesus tells us (Luke 20:38), "He is not
God of the dead, but of the living; for all live to him."